Not For Resale
THIS IS A FREE BOOK
bookthingbaltimore@hotmail.com
THE BOOK THING of BALTIMORE, INC.

THE BOOK THING OF BALTIMORE, INC.

THIS IS A FREE BOOK
www.bookthing.org

Not For Resale
THIS IS A FREE BOOK

bookthingbaltimore@hotmail.com
THE BOOK THING of BALTIMORE, INC.

BEIJING:
THE NEW FORBIDDEN CITY

BEIJING:
THE NEW FORBIDDEN CITY

SKYA GARDNER-ABBATE

Triple Tiger Tales
A Division of
Southwest Acupuncture College Press
Santa Fe, New Mexico

Published by Triple Tiger Tales
A division of Southwest Acupuncture College Press
1329 Acequia Borrada
Santa Fe, New Mexico 87501

Copyright © 1990 by Skya Gardner-Abbate
All rights reserved.

Cover and book design by Anthony Abbate

"Liberty artwork" for cover design courtesy of:
Jef Sharp, artist and Gravity Graphics Inc.
Copyright © 1989 by Gravity Graphics
All rights reserved.

Library of Congress Catalogue Card Number: 90-72130
ISBN 0-9628620-0-2

Printed in the United States of America
First Edition   1991

ACKNOWLEDGEMENTS

To the many selfless people who put our lives before their own in an ultimate gesture of good will, international peace, and common humanity. The names of our hosts and the places where our group stayed have either been omitted or changed in this book. To Sally Rudich, my copy editor, for her invaluable expertise and dedication in carefully helping me clarify my thoughts through the written word. To Anthony, my husband, for his unending patience and encouragement in my writing and, most of all, for his gift to me - China.

*From Tiananmen to Timisoara,
to freedom fighters everywhere.*

CONTENTS

FOUNDATION - PREFACE xix

FREEDOM 1

FASCINATION 5

FAMILIARIZATION 9

FOREWARNING 15

FEET FIRST 21

FLIGHT 25

FIRST IMPRESSIONS 31

FOOTLOOSE 35

FAIR WEATHER 43

FOREIGN DEVILS AND THE
    FIBER OPTIC NETWORK 49

FORTUNE 53

FORLORN 59

FISH STORIES AND THE FEAST 67

FLASHBACK 73

FLYING PIGEONS 79

FRIENDSHIP   83

FABLE   91

FRIVOLITY   97

FRENCH FRIES AND FALLEN DRAGONS   103

FERVOR   109

FOURTH OF JUNE   117

FIRE AND RAIN   125

FIRESIDE CHATS   131

FACADE   137

FRIEND OR FOE   143

FOREVER YOUNG   151

FORSAKEN   157

FELLOWSHIP   165

FOXHOLE IN FANTASY LAND   173

FRENZY   183

FAREWELL TO A FIELD OF DREAMS   193

FLYING TIGERS   197

FUTURE   201

FINALE - AFTER THE FALL FROM HEAVEN   205

FOOTNOTES   209

BEIJING:
THE NEW FORBIDDEN CITY

FOUNDATION

PREFACE

Beijing: The New Forbidden City

I visited China for the first time in May of 1988. During this six-week journey, I came to love the simplicity of life in that foreign land, where culture still seemed so connected to the fulfillment of basic needs, instead of the arbitrary and artificial, I thought, pursuit of personal happiness.

I was fascinated by the juxtaposition of past and present everywhere. Each morning, I marvelled to see the population of Beijing emerge through ornately-carved wooden doors, dilapidated reminders of centuries long gone, from modern chalky grey cinder-block compounds, to jump onto identical one-speed black bicycles that seemed to transport the city from the imperial past into the twentieth century. And I was immediately intrigued by the sound of the language, so unlike any of the six I had studied in my life.

One year later, on May 26, 1989, I left for another study tour in China, this time leading a group of seven students. Exactly one week before our departure, martial law had been imposed in Beijing in response to the pro-democracy movement initiated by university students in the spring of 1989 who were refusing to abandon their hunger strike in support of their dreams of freedom and equality for all. The declaration of martial law did not discourage us from our long-awaited trip, however. If anything, the excitement engendered by the evening news coverage encouraged us to embark.

Foundation - Preface

On May 28, just one week before the now famous Tiananmen Massacre, my friends and I visited the square to witness first-hand the hopes of freedom being born as China moved in the direction of democracy. For the rest of that week, long days of learning and exploring occupied our minds and exhausted our bodies, yet our thoughts were never far from the irrepressible youths who were testing the limits of their elders and their culture.

After the interminable night of horror on June 3, when untold numbers of students were killed at Tiananmen Square, my friends and I grieved in silence for three days, waiting to see how the Chinese and the entire world would respond to the slaughter. Due to the increasing gloominess of the political situation, and our own inability to provide any solace to our hosts, we decided to leave China on June 7. The next day we arrived back in San Francisco to a freedom newly cherished and never to be taken for granted.

What value this small work has other than to help me see these events as past, and to put them into perspective so as to propel future action, remains to be seen. That night, when I heard the bullets ringing and knew the government was turning on its own people, I wondered: Why isn't everyone who can hear this crying out? Why aren't they despairing? Why isn't the world outraged? Why isn't anybody doing anything?

I still wonder.

This book is my cry.

Skya Gardner-Abbate

FREEDOM

Beijing: The New Forbidden City

*L*ife would never be the same for us. Then again, who would want it to be? We were eight Americans studying in Beijing in the summer of 1989, too small in number to be rescued, too large in life to think there was no significance to our presence in that city during those times of life and death.

Modern day China had never been so free, so open, so euphoric as in that fateful June. Neither had it ever been so severely myopic that it would crush its own children rather than consider their demands. The onslaught, in its blind determination to maintain the status quo and prevent change, defiantly contested China's ancient philosophical heritage. Acting out of fear, the country's rulers ignored the natural law of growth and decay, their own legacy, where yielding is grounded in the recognition of the inevitable decline of all living things. It was both the best and the worst of times in China and we were there.

The tanks and bullets that paralyzed political and human growth along Chang'an Avenue, the Avenue of Eternal Peace, and at Tiananmen Square, the Square of Heavenly Peace, sent many to heaven that day. As I

Freedom

laid in the security of my dormitory on the eve of the massacre, listening to the Chinese being slaughtered outside my bedroom window, I felt the meaning of my own life come into sharper focus. Never again would I selfishly take my homeland's liberties for granted just because their maintenance did not require daily struggle or sublimation. For us as Americans, the violence at Tiananmen Square freed our political consciousness from its own confines.

This story is not an objective historical account of the turmoil that erupted in Beijing that summer, although everything in this recollection is true. Instead, it is a subjective interpretation of what those thirteen days meant to an American who, having travelled and studied in China the previous year, felt at home in a country as different from her homeland as night and day.

This time around, I was to leave that fatal shore forever changed. My first-hand witnessing of history brought into perspective the value of our precious American freedom of expression, and that is the tale I must tell.

FASCINATION

Beijing: The New Forbidden City

*L*ike many people in my generation, I had experienced a certain attraction to Eastern cultures during my younger years, but I had never dreamed that my path would take me 12,000 miles from home on more than one occasion to experience the warmth, generosity, naivete, and brutality that perhaps is not so much Chinese as it is human.

My first trip to Beijing in the summer of 1988 lasted six weeks. Anyone who knew me then could attest to the terror I experienced in journeying to that far-off land. Philosophically and professionally, I felt the need to travel to the country of my chosen occupation's beginnings; personally, I dreaded the changes in lifestyle I knew I would be bound to accommodate. Having previously lived in Brazil for a year and a half as a Peace Corps volunteer, I knew how difficult adjusting to another culture could be, even if it was only for a brief span of time. I surmised that the fulfillment of basic needs and the Chinese way of doing things would be even more difficult.

While the other fourteen people in my study group became intoxicated with the opportunity of visiting an exotic country, I reluctantly took on the journey

Fascination

only because I needed the knowledge I hoped such an experience would bestow. Ironically, as the days of our visit unfolded, many of these same friends became progressively disenchanted with the cultural reality we were to know as China, while I became hopelessly enamored of virtually everything Chinese! By the end of my stay, I even agreed that the "one" could be sacrificed for the "many" in the name of Communism, since this philosophy seemed to be working for the common good of the Chinese people. Little did I know then that beneath the expressionless faces that pressed against cloudy window panes of crowded buses or pedalled hypnotically down narrow lively streets, the longing to be free was already smoldering upon timbers of resignation and resentment.

FAMILIARIZATION

Beijing: The New Forbidden City

During that first visit, many magical days flowed one into another as I opened my mind to the city where I found myself transported and transformed. Strolling with friends in Beihai Park beneath a canopy of paper lanterns fashioned into fruits, sipping instant coffee at the Beijing Hotel, cheering the silliness of street acrobats, I took an incredible delight in the simplest of activities and felt a satisfied appreciation for the "here and now" of life. Even the basic need of eating took on new meaning; it was an act to be shared, an opportunity to revel in tastes and textures in a culture where you could be sure anything that was edible would be eaten.

Without the tool of language, however, the inner mind of our host country could only be conjectured, not explored. Several foreign friends, by their clever comments, were able to give us a glimpse of the Chinese world view. More often we tended to tread around the inner sanctums of personal experience for fear of being too invasive or impolite. The few caustic statements the dissident managed to opportunely express, such as, "Even pigs are given better food than that provided in the compound cafeteria for the workers," conveyed to us that the working people were regarded by the party as no

Familiarization

better than animals, at least in the minds of some Chinese.

Occupations were assigned according to perceived qualifications and the needs of the party; individual choice or the desire for personal fulfillment were not considered. The extended families that typified traditional Oriental life for so many centuries had been fragmented by the Communist party into smaller than nuclear units. It was common for college-educated individuals to become permanently estranged from their families once they were allotted a work position. A translator who wanted to be a travel agent bitterly divulged that "absence kills love" when we asked her about her family now thousands of miles away in southeast China. From a functionalist perspective, her rendering of our "absence makes the heart grow fonder" was a convenient slogan, but her distant eyes told me this popular adage was merely a sad culture-bound expression.

Marriages were still arranged and courtships encouraged accordingly in place of the perchance of romantic love. Then, after the thrown-together couple had had enough time to acquire at least mutual compatibility, it was not unusual for spouses to suffer long, obligatory separations from each other in the name of duty. Ultimately, delegated employment, arranged marriages, and mandatory estrangements made love and passion in any respect forbidden. The only glue of the social fabric was endurance.

Blank, impassive faces ignored us as we drove parallel to throngs of workers pedaling themselves to

11

their designated employment. Yet, curious street vendors would proudly proffer their regional cuisine and unabashedly watch as we devoured their food with great pleasure. Street food, which we had first avoided like the plague for fear of contracting illness, became our food of choice, superior even to the lavish Sunday brunch at the Great Wall Sheraton Hotel. We were pleased to let down our culinary guard in favor of experiencing the real China. Without language, our gusto, our consumption of the food, and our smiles conveyed to the street sellers our appreciation of their proud efforts.

The majority of the Chinese with whom we conversed expressed no desire to leave their motherland in the face of current conditions. They loved China and wanted to be with their families, and they hoped to help their country improve. Intensely proud of their homeland, most were as cognizant of its mammoth history as if it had occurred in their own personal lifetime. Their incredible love of this poor nation embarrassed me because I did not feel the same way about America. Nationalism was not in the forefront of my value system at that time. Little did I know then how much this was to change one year later during my second visit to China.

Upon my return to the United States a few days before the fourth of July in 1988, I had the impression that China was making headway in providing as equitably as possible for all of its citizens. My husband and I engaged in vigorous discussions that nearly turned into quarrels, where he felt we were privileged and lucky to be born in America and I felt it didn't matter because life in China, although hard, was worthwhile and what the

Familiarization

people really wanted. Without access to their language, the dreams of the Chinese populace were inscrutable to me. I had no way of recognizing their human longing for expression of a free spirit until the construction of a goddess of democracy before my very eyes just one year later shamed me into touch.

FOREWARNING

Beijing: The New Forbidden City

After my return from Beijing, I immediately told my husband I hoped to return to China with another study group in the coming year. In anticipation, I began to study the Chinese language. My group had not encountered any major problems in engaging in most of the basic activities we needed to do because of the availability of translators or people who spoke English. Still, I wanted to at least be able to speak the niceties, if not more, before embarking on my second trip to Beijing.

I also began to devour any books I could find on China, covering such diverse topics as Asian art, Chinese fairy tales, poems, literature, medical and historical works, and autobiographies. I felt driven to familiarize myself with anything that might give me insight into the Chinese mind.

Unquestionably, the most critical book that I read was the autobiography entitled <u>Life and Death in Shanghai</u> written by Nien Ching, a Shell Oil executive imprisoned and criticized during the Cultural Revolution, the history of which I knew next to nothing. Through her eyes I became exposed to a barbaric China, the antithesis of the kind and gentle people we had met at the hospitals. Certainly, she was not speaking of the

Forewarning

lighthearted vendors with whom we had flirted on street corners while buying them a round of beer! Yet it was certain from what I read that the majority of these acquaintances must have endured China's darkest period of cultural repression. In retrospect, the only explanation I could come up with was that these souls were in fact relatively content with their new social situations and therefore reluctant to articulate any discontent.

Completing the book, I experienced a profound sense of shock as I realized I had just visited and returned from a country so recently emerged from its brutal past. A portentous feeling came over me; I feared that the history of the Chinese was analogous to the movement of a pendulum; now the past might repeat itself since things were once again on the upswing. I shared this observation with a few people, particularly my close associates and China compatriots. For the ensuing year, I passionately prayed that my observation was an exaggerated and inaccurate historical assessment, but I found that I could never let go of the disturbing premonition.

Despite my readings, my infatuation with China did not diminish. Rather, I found it accelerating almost exponentially as my ethnocentrism decreased. The language I was studying became less foreign and my enthusiasm, which had been so lacking the previous year, only increased.

It wasn't until the following March, just two months before our next departure, that second thoughts once again began to stalk me. As much as I loved China, I remembered all of the things that made life hard and

Beijing: The New Forbidden City

dreary there, and I felt reluctant to give up my sunny, cheerful home for interminably polluted Beijing skies, inhospitable service people, and hostile taxi drivers.

Eventually, my dread subsided as I recalled the many experiences we had that affirmed life: waking up to old Chinese men and women singing outside my hotel window, doing voice *qi gong* to circulate their energy; riding a bike with an abandon I had never known as a child, and dancing to the top forties alongside Hong Kong and Taiwanese Chinese at the Holiday Inn. All of this, in concert with the astounding political events developing during April and particularly that May, generated an excitement about values more important than oneself. I pondered global issues, the bigger picture, and the question of what was the purpose of life beyond narrow personal ambitions.

The events in China escalated on the nightly news before the world's eyes. Significant history was clearly in the making. As I absorbed the media, I told myself that it would be a hospitable and curious period to be in China. Exactly one week before our departure, when the students in China were refusing to abandon their hunger strike, my sister telephoned and begged me not to go to Beijing. She was convinced that, with the edict of martial law in place, bloodshed was inevitable and we would become victims of being in the wrong place at the wrong time. I tried to assure her the Chinese people we had known were kind and gentle. Subliminally, I was well aware of the 4000 year saga of a warring nation, not to mention my own physically unpleasant personal experiences with angry pedicab and taxi driv-

Forewarning

ers who fought with me less than a year before over the price of a fare. But I reassured her that we would be prudent and not reckless as she continued in her efforts to convey to me the seriousness of my undertaking.

Recognizing the volatility of the situation, I knew if I truly appreciated my democratic freedoms, I would have to be prepared to demonstrate if asked. I simply could not go to China for my own personal reasons and ignore the larger issues at stake. If confronted, how could I shrug off the fact that students were willing to die for a political system they had heard was better than their own, a system I had the good fortune, as my husband pointed out, to enjoy? Was I only willing to selfishly reap the benefits of a democratic government without contributing to its survival? How could I not join in as these students starved themselves? My words of support for democracy would be hollow if I was not prepared to die for the freedoms that allow for the worldwide realization of humanity.

Upon hanging up the phone, I deeply considered the implications of my personal voyage to China, acknowledging a purpose greater than my own life. I walked into my bedroom, looked myself in the eye in our full-length mirror, and said, "Yes, if necessary, I am willing to die for these innate human rights." After that observation, my terror subsided and an excitement like I had never known mobilized me. I was ready to embark on the biggest sociological event of my life, a quest for meaning and significance superseding the spectrum of personal existence.

Beijing: The New Forbidden City

I packed my bags with eighteen colorful cotton outfits to get me through my anticipated two and a half week stay in Beijing. Matching socks, earrings, lipsticks, and light-weight jackets had all been carefully selected . Yet, I still felt something was missing. A nagging feeling nudged me to keep glimpsing at the digital clock glowing on my bedroom windowsill counting down the hours until departure. As time flipped by, I hesitantly informed my husband that I needed to go to the store, ostensibly to pick up a few last minute items. Was it just an uncontrollable desire to spend one last evening consuming that prompted me to go to the mall, or was I responding to apprehension about the trip? Underplaying their significance, I said I was looking for a pair of shoes that would go with all of my outfits so I wouldn't need to pack several pairs. More honestly, I wanted to find a pair of shoes for running, just in case we had to quickly get away from any situation.

Second, I wanted a new lipstick, the perfect shade to lend life to my face and uplift my spirits. I always buy lipstick when I'm anxious, an intrigue unconsciously cultivated since I was a child. My mother and sister feel the same way. No matter what time of day, what we are wearing, or how we are feeling we always felt better, brighter, more in control if we surrounded our lips with the brilliant moist colors nature has not ordained.

After casing the entire mall, and carefully comparing price, comfort, and style, I settled on an inconspicuous pair of white Calvin Klein tennis shoes. While I knew that white wasn't the most practical color to wear in industrially polluted Beijing, they certainly would match all of the clothing I had packed and, more importantly, they seemed to have that reassuring "at home" feeling that I could call upon in a foreign land. Plus, if I had to run, they were sure to stay on my feet.

That evening I couldn't wait to try out my new lipstick. To my surprise, the beauty of its color was only matched by the offensiveness of its unusual odor. Never before had I purchased a lipstick that smelled rancid! Shortly after sketching my lips, I felt a bad sore throat and swollen glands coming on. A bitter taste invaded my mouth. As I scrubbed off the sheer pigment, it occurred to me that this was not an auspicious harbinger of tomorrow. I hoped I wouldn't have to put the sneakers through a similarly disappointing test.

FLIGHT

MAY 26

Beijing: The New Forbidden City

At the San Francisco airport, no tears or fears accompanied my departure. I wasn't afraid of this second sojourn like I had been before my first trip to China when my husband had to practically push me through the gate leading to the plane, assuring me I would have the time of my life. Instead, an unwielding confidence and excitement infused me. I was feeling quite proud to be entrusted with the education and acculturation of the seven colleagues getting on the plane with me.

Soon we were racing over the ocean through a sky that never slept. The mood on the plane was ecstatic. Everyone was buzzing about what a propitious time it was to be travelling to China. Next to us, a young American history professor, who had hopes of securing a teaching position in one of Beijing's universities and felt compelled to experience this historical episode first-hand, glowed like a madonna with her newborn, such was her pride in the evolution of events. I envied her fluency with the language, her spontaneity, her sense of adventure, and her professional acumen. What fun it would be to have such potential for influence in the classroom, to be involved in the student movement! I

Flight

briefly wondered why I hadn't become a professor, an historian, a journalist, or a news reporter? A middle-aged Chinese couple sitting directly behind us described how they were forfeiting positions in a prestigious American university to take their skills back to China at a time when they thought they would be welcome. Overcome with the hope that their country was now about to embrace equality and prosperity for all, their smiling eyes danced seducing us all into the belief that significant social change was about to occur.

As if in affirmation, capitalism raised its indomitable head when the flight attendants began making their way up and down the aisles selling cartons of American cigarettes. The couple with whom we had spoken catapulted us into cascades of laughter when they frantically purchased several cartons of Marlboros for friends only to hastily exchange them when word circulated that Camels were now the "in" tobacco. Disoriented from jet-lag and inebriated with anticipation, we tried to mentally calculate how much cash was brought in that night and to whom the money would be going, only to abandon the exercise in favor of silently savoring the dissonance of East meeting West before our very eyes.

Eighteen hours later we were ushered into China through murky skies. Humanity's odors greeted us at the Shanghai airport, our place of entry to the country but not our final destination. For about an hour, we restlessly scrutinized the humid, dreary terminal, searching for signs of the student movement. Racehorses darting across the overhead television monitor in the lounge didn't give us any clues. While waiting to reboard the plane bound for Beijing, we were accosted by a serious six-year-old Chinese boy making his way from seat to seat, surveying Americans about life in the United States with an urgency that suggested his own life might soon be in transition. He was clearly not as impressed with us as we were with his near-perfect English and penetrating questions about whether we ate a lot of bread or had a telephone in every house. As his proud young father escorted the precocious child on his rounds, I was moved by the obvious love and delight beaming on the older man's already worn face, expressing the pride Chinese so typically feel about their children. Today, I can't help but wonder if this discerning boy's existence will be any easier, whether it will ever match the hopeful expectations expressed in his loving father's eyes.

FIRST IMPRESSIONS

MAY 27

Beijing: The New Forbidden City

*I*n light of recent political developments, we had no idea what to expect when we arrived in Beijing. The familiar American Express billboard hovering over the entrance to the baggage claim area encouraged me to think at least some things hadn't changed. But my luggage, last to arrive, somehow forewarned things would not be easy for us.

Shortly after clearing customs, just as we began to chase down taxi drivers, we were rescued by our Chinese hosts. Their friendly faces and excellent English reassured me everything was fine; we had not made the wrong decision in coming to China. Once the luggage was stowed in the school van and we had perched our adrenaline-steeped bodies upon them, we were expediently escorted into the heart of Beijing. Speeding down the moonlit boulevard, ignoring the warning of red lights, we looked askance at each other as if to ask, "Is anything possible here?"

Although it was well past midnight, the silhouettes of lone bicycle riders floated on top of the tall trees lining the airport road. At one intersection, our careening bus was halted by a small group of men who quickly inspected our vehicle and then released us. When we

First Impressions

asked our Chinese guide if they were students policing the streets, he replied that it was hard to tell, but gave no indication that this activity was out of place. He explained that some groups who did not have the privilege of being students, yet identified with the pro-democracy movement, had assumed these vigilante roles.

From running the red lights to the self-appointed rogues, unusual nighttime activity in a city that normally slept by 10 P. M. hinted that the daily matrix of life in Beijing had been altered by recent events on the square and something more encompassing than a student movement was underway.

FOOTLOOSE

MAY 28

Beijing: The New Forbidden City

Sunday morning opened to a muggy, overcast Beijing. My skittish students wanted to immediately get out of the dorm and see China. I stalled them as long as possible in the interest of a good night's sleep; after all, I had done this before. Little did they know that while I cherished my rest, once I got going I would become indefatigable.

When we finally did get going, I practically had to restrain some members of our group from running. We made our way from our sleepy little compound to the bustle of the main thoroughfare, one block parallel to our residence. Needing Chinese money, we decided to begin our day by going downtown to exchange American dollars for FEC, the official foreign exchange currency. We situated ourselves at the closest bus stop and watched for the bus number our host had told me would take us to the Beijing Hotel where we planned to convert our money. But, in the early morning hours, I had forgotten to ask our host one important question: Which side of the street should we stand on?

While the heat of the day and hunger began to gnaw at us, the students took in the hubbub of the street for the first time and I tried to figure out which way was downtown. The previous year I had lived in a hotel with red velvet walls (surrounded by a canal in which human excrement floated) and learned my way to the city from that citadel, but I was lost when it came to determining the exact location of our present accommodations. As program director, I was forced to put shyness aside and walk over to the traffic station conveniently located across from the intersection where we were standing. Here I constructed my first complete Chinese sentence not memorized from my studies. Not quite knowing what was going to come out of my mouth, I exaggeratedly drawled, *"Ni hao. Wo xiang yao gonggongqichi yi ling yi."* (Hello, I would like the 101 bus.) To my surprise, the traffic officer responded animatedly, alternately pointing to the place where we were initially standing and then to the opposite side of the street. But I had no idea what she said. My impression was that the 101 bus could be picked up on either side of the route; where to catch it just depended upon which direction one was going. I already knew that.

My student companion who had accompanied me to the station looked at me in awe as sounds even stranger than my usual New England accent spilled from my mouth. I may have impressed her and established my position of leadership, but we still didn't know on which corner to stand to catch the bus. Where we had been standing before didn't quite correspond with our interpretation of the map, so we opted to pick up the bus on the opposite side of the street. But now all the 101's we saw going our way were full and would not stop.

Beijing: The New Forbidden City

    We decided to walk west. After about five minutes of skirting bicycles and baby carriages, we arrived at a familiar crossroads. A woman, who spoke English and heard us deliberating about which of the several bus stops to stand at, helpfully designated the bus that would take us to the center of Beijing. Like standing sardines, we scrunched and swayed on the bus for two long blocks before the bus driver abruptly stopped at what was apparently the end of the route, screeching that everyone must get off.

    Unable to discern what had happened or why, we found ourselves in front of the landmark Kentucky Fried Chicken, within view of the palatial Peace Hotel. Since all hotels have money exchanges, we decided to cash our travellers' cheques there. A quick lesson in Chinese currency ensued. With money to spend, we were ready to feast so we decided to check out the costly buffet at the Peace Hotel. Instead of dining there, we agreed to continue as planned to the Beijing Hotel for a Chinese lunch.

    Outside the Peace Hotel, I negotiated reasonable rates from two taxi drivers to take our group to the downtown hotel on Chang'an Avenue. Within seconds of getting into the vehicles, the taxis returned to the route where the bus had abandoned us, only to become ensnared in a traffic jam unusual even for a city the size of Beijing. Just to show off, I thought I'd try out one of my little slang phrases while we were at a standstill. *"Zenme le?"* (What's wrong?) I queried. Both my friends' and the taxi driver's mouths dropped open as if to say, "You can speak Chinese!" My brazenness backfired when the taxi driver babbled back his quick response and I was left at a loss. Laughingly, I admitted to my companions that although I could speak a little of the language, I could rarely decipher a reply. However, I was satisfied with my ability to be understood which prompted me to be even more adventurous.

Once inside the dining room of the historic hotel, I relished the familiarity of a steaming bowl of noodles and chicken followed by gratifying gulps of cold Coca Cola. In a flash, I savored the memory of my first Coca Cola in China the year before. Together, a friend and I had sat in the Emperor's garden of the Forbidden City sipping warm cokes under the protection of an ancient gnarled tree, as the gentle summer rain fell upon us and hundreds of Chinese citizens, sheltered beneath the imperial eves of glazed tile, regarded us. We all seemed to epitomize the Chinese advertisement for the soft drink: "Delicious, Be Happy." This year, as the students' guide into Chinese culture and cuisine, I hoped their experiences would be as simple and satisfying as the remembered coke motto promised.

Ordering in a Chinese restaurant, like doing almost anything in China, can be a lesson in frustration and tolerance. What better time to experience it than on one's first day! Surrounded by a half dozen disinterested waiters in the otherwise empty auditorium-like dining room, we awkwardly ordered from the one menu our table was offered. Explaining dishes and their cost in FEC and equivalent dollar amounts, I tried to instruct my friends in the skills and food selections that would ensure their survival in the city without me after I left them midway through the trip.

We waited with varying degrees of amusement and satisfaction. Soon, dish by dish, our meals began to emerge from the kitchen. Some people got what they ordered, others got more, some got none — that was the Beijing Hotel. After enough beer and soda, even the more resistant began reveling in the "here and now" of life, one of the particular reasons I loved China so much. This land, so different from other foreign countries I had known, so discontinuous with my past, made me feel utterly liberated. No roles or expectations confined me, except the pleasant position of program director. It was a place for me to discover my unconstrained self, a place to suspend the routines that were the comfortable boundaries of my life at home. To me, this was the biggest gift that China had to offer, an attraction ultimately more important than our actual studies. Little did we know that in exactly one week we would have the opportunity to discover the deepest meaning of our lives in an unexpected but inescapably Chinese context.

FAIR WEATHER

Beijing: The New Forbidden City

Finishing our lunch, we were fueled and ready for adventure. As we left the colossal hotel, we encountered a parade making its indubitable way to Tiananmen Square. The procession marched past us obstructing traffic with calligraphic banners, bright flags, and loud speakers. It didn't take us long to get caught up in the excitement, and soon we were headed down the broad boulevard in the same direction, hiding behind trees and each other, fearing that our cameras might be confiscated while we surreptitiously snapped pictures.

    Before we knew it, we had walked to the entrance of the closed Forbidden City, guarded by Mao's aloof visage and located directly across from Tiananmen Square. To reach the square, we had to go by way of an underground passage. We encountered a number of sprawling, thin, tired students seeking refuge from the sun in the tunnel. They seemed to view us with hope, their desperate hungry eyes reaching out as we filed past them. We emerged from the tunnel stripped of timidity and infused with animation to confront the brilliant, incongruous glory of tents pitched on the concrete floor of Tiananmen Square, the Square of Heavenly Peace.

Fair Weather

The last time I had been to Tiananmen Square was one year before when my roommate and I, skipping class, braved bruises, bicycle grease, and brutal temperatures to visit this historic site before returning to the United States. With schoolgirl glee, we giggled and posed coquettishly, snapping pictures of each other in front of the monuments. As our final formal goodbye to China, we had traversed the width and length of the flat expanse, recounting the tale of the role it had played in history and the blood that had been shed beneath our feet. Little did we know then that the same slabs would bear witness to another scene of Chinese carnage one year later. It seemed ironic then as it does now that the Square of the Heavenly Peace should commemorate an illusionary peace at best.

Slowly creeping closer to the center of the square, we incredulously asked ourselves how we had actually dared to enter that sanctum, so publicly associating ourselves with the student movement? We evaded the tents of young students squatting amid pots, pans, and sleeping bags, and the neat medical tents stationed by middle-aged doctors whose tense and wearied faces conveyed the rigor of their commitment and the seriousness of their undertaking. With the excuse that we did not want to be intrusive by weaving in and out amongst the private living quarters, we recognized only two alternatives — leave or advance to the center of the activity.

Only seconds elapsed before we were close to the cordoned off monument, the focal point of the square. Conspicuous with our blond hair, sneakers, shorts, and cameras, we soon became the vortex of a formidable crowd. In typical youthful American fashion, we spoke and gestured with exhilaration, exclaiming that democracy was good and freedom inalienable, and that the whole world had their eyes on China. The poorly dressed students, infatuated with the concept, egged us on until we became uncomfortable, realizing the eyes of the entire world could be upon us.

As we started to scatter, we were beckoned to step over the cable fence and make our way up to the monument. There, international photographers were furiously flashing pictures while student leaders surveyed the crowd and loud speakers blared. Lifting our legs over the cordon leading to the vantage point of the square was a substantial step. My whiny protest, that I wasn't convinced I wanted to be so visible, was barely heard in the short amount of time it took for everything to ensue. Summoned and pushed, we automatically crossed over in single file, not unlike Jews consciously marching to their deaths, I imagined. What was driving us? Desire or destiny?

*FOREIGN DEVILS
AND THE
FIBER OPTIC NETWORK*

Beijing: The New Forbidden City

*O*nce within the confines of the cordon, we were informed by students who spoke English that we could join the photographers on the steps of the monument if we had a press card. One of my friends had recently received the newly issued telephone charge *FON* card just before leaving the states. With lightning-like alacrity, I jokingly suggested that we could say we were from a fictitious press, the "Fiber Optic Network," and get away with it. As much out of nervousness as hilarity, we decided to enjoy the ploy amongst ourselves, but not tempt fate any further. We were daring enough to show our support by our presence on the square, conscientious enough to grant the Chinese the right to self-determination, and sober enough to be concerned about our own safety. We hadn't even been in China twenty-four hours and we were already stretching the limits of our own daring. Considering what was to yet to come in Beijing, it was none too soon to learn how to access our wisdom and courage.

Conspicuously inhabiting a no-man's land somewhere between the masses and the monument, we moved like lemmings to the east of the square while a staccato speech serenaded the Sunday summer afternoon. Avert-

Foreign Devils and the Fiber Optic Network

ing my eyes from the curious crowds on the steps of the People's Mansion, I looked up at the sky and saw the massive painting of Mao Tse Tung crowning the rouge-red entrance to the Forbidden City. The haughty portrait seemed to glare at us inhospitably as if to ask, "What right have you "foreign devils" being in China, let alone outside the walls of the Forbidden City?!" Mao's icy, superior countenance did not seem to bestow benignancy upon the people within its glance.

In fact, his secret smile gave us the distinct impression that we were being watched and some of my friends reported they had seen conspicuous looking men snapping pictures of us as we rallied in the square. At that moment, it was as if the alluring Forbidden City, captured so eloquently in the motion picture The Last Emperor, extended its towering feudal walls to surround the entire city of Beijing. Indeed, it seemed Beijing had become the New Forbidden City.

FORTUNE

Beijing: The New Forbidden City

As the crowd waned, so did our energy. Like veterans, we trudged back to the Beijing Hotel for a refreshing round of drinks and a rest. The massive hotel was remarkably empty. We quickly scanned the gift stalls in the stately lobby on our way to the lounge. Seating ourselves, we established our own sphere for socializing, ordering cold beer, soft drinks, and coffee in a disorganized fashion, much to the aggravation of our diffident waiters. After luxuriously languishing over our last sips, we were ready to resume our touring.

Next, we took a cab to the Friendship Store, about a half mile away, where we surveyed the goods for future shopping and picked up treats to stow in our rooms for breakfast or snacking. A quick scurry in the supermarket section provided bottled water, juices, biscuits, tea and Snickers bars—enough food to last a few days. Since we found ourselves just one block west from the best shopping turf in town, the "bazaar" as I called it, we decided to examine the goods there as well as engage in the black market, converting our foreign exchange currency to "*renminbi*," the peoples' money.

Changing money on the black market was highly lucrative though it was illegal. For every FEC, one could receive one and a half *renminbi*, the money in which the natives transacted. Even though it is illegal for foreigners to be caught trading FEC for *renminbi*, it is legal for them to use *renminbi*. Yet, taxis, hotels, and certain stores and restaurants will only accept FEC from foreigners so we did not want to convert all of our FEC. Different money is used for different things and so a tourist must have both on hand for the appropriate opportunity. Many visitors who are passing through the city never use anything other than FEC, popularly called "new money" by the Chinese. However, students and shoppers who stay for longer periods of time often convert their FEC to *renminbi*, referred to as "old money," to make it stretch further.

To a fairly conservative person like myself, changing money sounded dangerous — for about one week, that is. The prospect of expanding one's buying power, not to mention the excitement of a dangerous encounter, proved irresistible to this confederate shopper as well as the rest of the group.

Entrepreneurs eager to change money were everywhere, particularly around entrances to hotels and shopping districts patronized by foreigners. As we walked past bushes and vending stalls, merchants would coo, "Change money, change money," perhaps the only English they knew, but unmistakably the magic words. Outsiders coveted the "old money" so they could purchase more goods at already dirt cheap prices, and natives craved the "new money" so they could convert it into dollars to be sent to relatives in the United States. They also used it to procure cherished items in popular demand on the black market, like color television sets and refrigerators.

The general rule of thumb was to exchange money only in clandestine spheres where one felt safe and only with trusted patrons who would pay the prevalent exchange rate. Skinny, shifty-eyed teenagers and unctuous "social youths" were ignored in place of middle-aged, trustworthy grandparent-type vendors with whom we felt an affinity. The strategic course of action was to stroll up and down the narrow corridor of the open air market, casually browsing at goods while getting a sense of the person and their exchange rate which often differed from stall to stall. Decisions to act were usually spontaneous. Suddenly, a friend flipping through piles of silk underwear would be adroitly absorbed into a tiny booth crammed with sleeping children, spouses, and parents, blankets, tea kettles, and mounds of backstocked merchandise.

Within a short amount of time, all eight of us had successfully converted a fair amount of our recently acquired colorful FEC for stacks of worn, wide wrinkled bills. As if a small miracle had occurred, we watched our money get transformed, not unlike the multiplication of loaves and fishes, into a small fortune. With each transaction from crisp travellers' cheques to *renminbi*, the money got older and dirtier, but more abundant. Unconventional scenes of the Forbidden City and portraits of proud workers, farmers, and skilled laborers replaced the aristocracy depicted on American dollars. Amazed by the colors, textures, pictures, and most of all the size of the bundles of bills, we felt we were endowed with play money for the duration of our stay. A corresponding attitude of adventure made us feel that whatever we wanted was ours for the asking and, later during our last days in China, for the giving.

FORLORN

MAY 29

Beijing: The New Forbidden City

Sunday proved to be an extremely satisfying day. The students had successfully acquired the skills of converting money and ordering in a restaurant, plus they were oriented to the city and the compound where we were staying. We had visited the major shopping districts including the Friendship Store, the bazaar, and the wonderful Wanfujing Street where everything imaginable could be secured. We had taken taxis and bustling buses. And we had firmly located the critical watering holes at each end of town, the Beijing Hotel and the Jianguo Hotel, both offering necessary oases of air conditioning, clean restrooms, and cool drinks to be utilized between frenzied shopping sprees.

Firsthand, we had visited the square, the center of student activity, to reassure ourselves that everything was "okay," as our Chinese host had told us upon our arrival in Beijing. We could now write home on postcards of pandas and Buddhas to let worried relatives know that the world within the Great Wall was safe and we would have a memorable trip.

The start of our serious training in medicine began Monday morning when the "whoosh" of corridor curtains opened at 5:00 in the morning sent a contingent

Forlorn

of students heading towards a nearby park to do Tai Ji exercises with the local population. I remained in my bed until about 6:00 A.M., my usual time to get up in China. Although I could not see them, I heard birds avidly chirping in the trees outside my bedroom window, heralding the arrival of the new day. There was no doubt in my mind that they sang in Chinese, such were the intonations and lilt in their high-pitched fragile voices. The sounds of the morning, like the sound track in a Chinese movie, never failed to remind me that I was in China.

    Alone in the room after my roommate left to exercise in the park, I studied our humble quarters. Our beds were heavenly and I always looked forward to a good night's sleep in my cozy little corner. The room was totally adequate to meet our needs, yet it lacked light because of a brick building that was about nine feet away from our window. The absence of sunshine and the obscurity of the sky slightly depressed me. Acclimated to the pristine clarity of Santa Fe, New Mexico skies, I knew this room could only serve as a refuge for me at night when the absence of natural daylight wouldn't bother me.

    The entire alcove was appointed with blond wooden furniture, a style I had thought so modern in the '60's in my favorite aunt's house. Everything was covered with an almost imperceptible layer of black soot, an inescapable facet of life in Beijing. Even though we were in a building that was only one year old, the wall to wall carpet was threadbare and, it appeared, selectively vacuumed. As a friend of mine so aptly summarized,

"The Chinese are tidy but not clean." There is a difference.

The bathroom was undoubtedly the oddest chamber I had ever seen; certainly not Kublai Khan's stately pleasure dome but perhaps to the Chinese it was a jade palace. After stepping up about a foot, one entered a wall-to-wall-to-floor green plastic enclosure. A dim light bulb made the already serpentine color of the smooth synthetic walls a more perverse shade of green. Looking in the mirror, faces, eyes, and teeth gleamed back an awful hue, making us feel like we had contracted a rare disease. Since no shower curtain hung on the curtain bar, a steaming torrent of water would not only make the walls appear to sweat with slime, but the floor would likewise acquire a marsh-like quality. Despite the strange decor, I was immeasurably grateful, just so we had a toilet, warm running water, and a shower. The tepid water that awaited us each morning and evening was refreshing after the grime and sweat engendered during ninety-degree-plus temperatures. We were all well aware that most of these luxuries would never be experienced by the average Chinese in their own homes.

I began to feel slightly depressed by the dreariness of the day and waking alone. Last year, I had loved to open the heavy double lined curtains that separated our lives from the rest of Beijing, sip hot tea, and eat raisin biscuits as the thin white morning light snuck through the window with the sounds of the waking world wafting up to our fifth floor hotel room. I would peer into the secret life of the family who lived next to the hotel behind the taxi station with endless fascination. Every morning, while I put on my eye shadow and dried my hair, I would see them come out and perform their morning rituals of washing dishes, dumping water, relieving themselves, and cuddling their children. Then they would pick up their rusty old bikes, head out the gate, and start off down the muddy, pot-holed street to their assigned destinations.

No human activity greeted me this morning as I carefully dressed, straightened my belongings, and organized the denominations and types of money I had accrued. Skipping breakfast, I met the students and our Chinese host outside the dorm at the appointed 7:45 A.M. departure time. Much to my dismay, my charges were rapidly whisked away from me by the mini-van heading to the hospital, while I was left behind to go through the formalities of meeting the teachers and the heads of the institute. Feeling lost and estranged, I dismally waved good-bye to their bright excited faces, regretting that I would not have the pleasure of watching them experience their first magical day inside a Chinese hospital.

With utmost respect, I was escorted into the guest lounge of the academy, presented with steaming hot jasmine tea, and introduced to all of the significant personages associated with the school. Abundant nods, smiles, and handshakes greeted me as director of our program. Attempting to convey my appreciation for their graciousness and the fact that I remembered them from last year, I feebly pieced together phrases from the selected vocabulary I had memorized. Even the eldest member of the group could not help choking with laughter over my pronunciation and sentence construction, but his smiling black eyes shimmered acknowledging my well-intentioned gestures.

Formalities were quickly over and I was on my own for the next three hours until the students returned. Not quite knowing what to do with my unplanned time, I took a short stroll around the compound, smiling sheepishly at anyone who passed. All too quickly, I found myself back in the dreary dorm. Thinking I could take a little nap, I laid down on the bed to rest. However, I wasn't tired, so I lingered silently in the room wondering what to do, listening to the children in the school adjacent to the dorm dancing to a scratchy record of *Jingle Bells*. When their delightful squeals ended, the drone of vacuum cleaners and women's voices echoed down the hall, getting louder as the approaching women jangled keys and slammed bedroom doors. Being a fanatic for cleanliness, I didn't want to forfeit the chance that our room might get cleaned, so I dressed quickly, gathered my Chinese language books and tapes, and departed to study in the student lounge of the academy. I should have known better though: having arrived only last night there was little chance our rooms would get tidied before next week.

Just as I was leaving, I heard the women scream and call out to each other and I knew they must have discovered Stan and Gigi's beds pushed together. In a country where it used to be against the law to rearrange state-owned furniture, I chuckled, knowing the women were cackling about more than just one impropriety.

FISH STORIES AND THE FEAST

Beijing: The New Forbidden City

*A*fter two hours of concentrated study, sipping aromatic tea, and observing the orientation of new students to the school, I was happy to hear my fledglings return. Rushing down the stairs, I met them as they scrambled off the bus, their chatter quickly revealing their enthrallment with the first day in the hospital. I knew all about the excitement they were experiencing: It was for this that we had journeyed to China.

Waiting to go to lunch, we milled outside the institute, basking in the noonday sunlight and relishing the afterglow of a satisfying morning. The first day of clinic seemed a reliable indicator of how the rest of the educational venture would go and I was pleased that the group was not disappointed.

Soon it was time to board the bus for the exclusive restaurant where we would dine. On this formal first day of our program it would not be just an ordinary meal. To initiate us into native culture and hospitality, we had been invited in customary tradition to a Chinese banquet. Remembering how the year before I had dreaded the unknown delicacies served to us at our first Chinese feast, I tried to prepare the students for the dining

Fish Stories and the Feast

experience in store for them. This year, my mouth was already salivating with the promise of boiled peanuts, braised chicken, and Peking duck, and I described our upcoming eating adventure with pleasant anticipation. Surrounded by Chinese students, doctors, and the directors of the Beijing program, about twenty of us filled two large round tables in a private dining room of a well-known roast duck restaurant. As leader of the program this year, I knew I was expected to give a toast, so I had studied my language lessons all morning trying to synthesize a small speech in Chinese as a token of our sincerity. At the opening of the banquet, without the aid of a translator, I nervously stood and spoke to my colleagues and hosts: "We are very pleased to be here. We are very happy to study acupuncture. We love China. Thank you very much." Knowing that the speech barely conveyed my message, I blushed self-consciously while our Chinese hosts politely applauded and chortled. My students couldn't understand what I said, but their rapt faces praised me anyway, for my courage if not for my language skills.

Formalities aside, the festivities began and one bizarre dish after another was brought from the kitchen. I showed the students at my table how to serve the choicest tidbits to the hosts sitting by our sides and, in turn, how to let themselves be served. The majority of the dishes I knew only by sight and smell, not by name. Throughout my life, I had always been wary of trying new foods, opting for the predictable over the promise of a new taste treat. But last year I had learned to love the food in China, so I wanted to try everything this time —

69

well, just about everything. I still didn't like the look of those black aspic eggs, although everyone said they tasted exquisite.

I reminded my students of what a friend of mine had pointed out to me before I left for Beijing. He believed that one needed to eat the food of a people to experience their consciousness. Swallowing this sage sociological advice, I encouraged everyone to savor the same strange foods I had smugly set aside the previous year. Sea cucumbers, fried hummingbird fetuses, garlic shoots, and fresh water carp were all generously sampled. I chuckled as I watched some of my students disdainfully dally with their food, taking only the daintiest bites with their chopsticks, while others daringly dove into platefuls of unknown delicacies.

At one point in the presentation of the fare, when a large dish of shining white strips swimming in a clear starchy sauce was served, an interesting discussion ensued. Helping ourselves, we curiously asked our hosts what we were eating. One of the doctors said it was a bean that was processed and sliced into the narrow slivers; another said it was a type of vegetable. We all nodded, commenting, "Oh, interesting," as we continued to nibble. Shaking their heads knowingly, the elder doctors sitting next to me resumed their zestful conversation. Finally, the translator broke into the table's chatter to proudly announce that these were not vegetables or beans. This succulent dish was no less than sharks' lips.

"Sharks' lips? The fish?" we asked incredulously. "Yes, we understood! Weren't they good?" they replied.

Fish Stories and the Feast

The students sitting with me smiled drunkenly, while all I could picture were enormous silver fish with their stereoscopic eyes swimming silently in large aquariums, conspicuously devoid of their sensuous, slimy lips as they peered out of their glass entrapment. And to top it off, the dish was delicious!

FLASHBACK

MAY 31

Beijing: The New Forbidden City

A few months prior to my first passage to Beijing, the prospective students going on the study program attended an orientation lunch with our program director, Jake Fratkin, who had lived in China for six months. Exceedingly pragmatic, Jake laid out a vivid description of what to expect in China. While he knew the hospital program would sound exciting, he also understood how important support systems would be during our six-week stay, so he clearly elucidated a more day-to-day version of Chinese life. This was the part I really feared: the food, the bathrooms, the language that didn't even sound human, and getting places by bicycle.

A friend of mine who had studied in Shanghai graphically described how the Chinese would gather around her in the unavoidable open-air bathrooms, as if her excrements would somehow be different from theirs. It all sounded like too much for me, a person who is very particular and accustomed to a husband who will do anything to make my life easier.

I was pleased with the turnout for the luncheon and how Jake inspired the students, but I was upset with myself. I felt that I didn't have the resiliency to go on the trip. Walking back to the car in the gusty wind, I

Flashback

vehemently disclosed to my husband, "Don't tell anybody yet, but I'm not going on the trip." I could not envisage myself on a bicycle riding elbow to elbow down the street alongside buses, taxis, and a motley assortment of other vehicles. Not perceiving myself as an athletic or adventuresome type, I didn't think I would be able to negotiate my way through the streets and keep up with everyone. All I could imagine was that I would be tired, hot, irritable, and inept. And I could not fathom people peering at me when I went to the bathroom! So, that was it — I couldn't go.

But of course I did. And one of the students and I purchased a bike together. Our Chinese host graciously assisted us at the bike store, helping with the language difficulties encountered in the transaction. Considering the duration of our stay, she ascertained that it would be cheaper to buy bikes outright and sell them back to the store where we bought them, rather than rent them on a daily basis.

At the bicycle store, we were promised via our Chinese aid that the more money we spent on a bike, the better the trade-in value would be. If I was going to have a bike, I insisted on a girl's, anticipating having to frequently jump off of it until my motor skills improved. I knew it would take awhile to learn how to move with the stream of black vehicles, literally the pulse of the city, flowing incessantly through the heart of the capital. Girls' bikes were harder to find and, since we wanted to make all of our purchases as a group to facilitate bringing the bikes back, I was forced to pay a premium price. A student and I shared the purchase of a deluxe woman's three-speed bike for 280 yuan, or about $75.00 (U.S.). At the end of our six-week stay, we sold it back to the same bicycle shop for about 160 yuan, making the cost of the bike roughly $20.00 apiece for the entire stay.

It took me three weeks to get on the bike that summer of 1988. My roommate, who craved physical activity, would gently prod me into going shopping by bike instead of by taxis which were extremely difficult to snag on the outskirts of Beijing. Using any excuse I could, I would decline demurely, but eventually it was my turn to compromise, and so I was baptized into the art of bicycle riding in China.

Just as I had been the last one to find a bike, I was also the last one to successfully sell mine back. Anticipating negotiations, I started with a ridiculously high bargaining price. My Chinese doctor friend dutifully translated my asking price with more passion than I had seen evidenced in the six weeks I had known her. Taken aback, I looked at her in surprise as she argued my case. The bike vendor listened to her proposition and shook his head. Finally, he asked how she, a Chinese woman, could be on the side of an American. Both became quite angry. Not wanting to cause her any discomfort, I quickly acquiesced to his buying price, but I was hurt that his nationalist attitude had interfered. I didn't want to be an ugly American, but I also wasn't going to be taken for a fool by failing to participate in the traditional bargaining practice.

The bike vendor asked my name as he made out the receipt. In Chinese, my name translates into "*Huayuan Tian*," Heavenly Flower Garden. I loved to go

Flashback

by this alias rather than my English name because I felt I had discovered another facet to my personality in China that was captured in the sound of *"Tian,"* meaning sky or heaven. Bewildered that this brazen American preferred a Chinese appellation to her own, the shop owner softly caressed the words, commenting on what a beautiful name it was. A moment later, he quickly caught my smiling eye and said the name did not suit me because of the way I had fought for my money.

Not only did I find cycling to be great fun and a pleasant mode of exercise, it was also the best way to get around the flat metropolitan expanse of Beijing without troublesome taxis, crowded buses, or confusing subterranean subways. By the time my 1989 trip rolled around, I was as psyched about getting a bike as most of the students in our group.

FLYING PIGEONS

Beijing: The New Forbidden City

We returned to the same bike store to do business again. This time the shop happened to be within convenient walking distance of our residence. We descended upon the sleepy little store to find the sales people lolling in the afternoon sun, lazily dangling cigarettes from their toothless mouths. Like children in a toy shop, eight anxious Americans filled the cement-floored store jammed full of poorly manufactured but shiny new red and blue bikes. We also found used, dusty, reliable black *Flying Pigeons*, the top of the line in English bicycles. Students zipped the bikes under consideration out of the store and onto the pavement to check brakes, tires, and steering. A group of men loitering outside the shop scooted themselves onto stairs to watch the parade of foreigners assiduously inspecting and trying out the bikes. Caught up in the novelty, they shouted out their advice: "Good bike." "Take it." "Buy mine here. It's better. Cheaper." Laughing, we friskily shouted back even though we knew they couldn't understand our responses.

We all loved our carefully selected new bikes. I found a sturdy expensive girl's bike again, a handsome Flying Pigeon with the word **Tianjin** inscribed on it in

Flying Pigeons

gold paint. Since part of my name, *"Tian,"* was on it, I immediately felt this bike had to be mine and I decided right then and there that I wanted to take it back to the states. A student promised to help me disassemble and pack it when the time came.

We spent another half hour in the shop filling tires with air, adjusting brakes and bike seats, and purchasing baskets, locks, and bells. Then we were ready to fly. Triumphantly, we emerged from the dingy bike store, walking alongside our prized possessions until we reached a street where we hopped on them like trusty mounts selected for a crusade. We could now let ourselves be absorbed into city life through the mainstream of street activity. We were one with the people!

FRIENDSHIP

Beijing: The New Forbidden City

Not more than five minutes elapsed before one of the students had to stop to have his brakes fixed. Like planes unable to land, we made circles around the busy intersection, waiting to proceed as a group to the bookstores and medical supply houses next on our day's agenda. Somehow, when we crossed the converging traffic, my girlfriend Dairne and I became estranged from the group. We looked for the others everywhere hoping they were also looking for us. Alternately heading north, south, east, and west, we searched for the bright clothing and colorful backpacks that would distinguish the students from the rushing current of commuters. Soon we realized it was a lost cause.

Undaunted, we decided to make the most of the day and our new found freedom. We were only concerned that our friends would worry about us. Since there was nothing we could do to locate them, we continued south down Dongshi Beidajie to its intersection with Chang'an Avenue, the pivotal axis leading to all of the places we loved to haunt. Furthermost to the left was the Jianguo Hotel, the bazaar, and the Friendship Store. To the right, Wanfujing Street, the Beijing Hotel, and the threatened Tiananmen Square beckoned.

Friendship

Dairne and I had a wonderful time that afternoon. I introduced her to the sparkling cool lounge of the Jianguo Hotel, where we enjoyed a toast of cold drinks, hers beer and mine Coke, before beginning our trek. Sprawling in the elegant bar outside the grasp of the broiling sun, we let the welcome air conditioning seep into our skin. Each moment was precious. Outside the luxurious shelter, we would be sweltering within minutes, as if we had never known the relief of the hotel or the cold beverages.

Our afternoon was filled with fun adventures as we searched the vendors' stalls at the bazaar adjacent to the ritzy hotel catering to foreigners. Looking for gifts for friends and bargains for ourselves, we ran each other ragged. As it approached 5:00 P.M. and we realized how fatigued and hungry we were, we agreed it was time to return to campus and find our friends.

Earlier that day when we first mounted our bikes, we were fresh and enthusiastic and the traffic flow was light. By the time we began heading back, we found ourselves amidst the working population of Beijing. I had biked in heavy traffic before and for much longer distances, but these particular three miles were harrowing. Elbow to elbow, three to five deep, we pedaled in first gear away from downtown and back to the dormitory. The only thing that saved me was my steel-like will. Even Dairne, who was an athlete in tip-top shape, had to muster all of her attention to keep up with the mass movement.

When I sneaked an insecure glance her way and saw that maneuvering was not easy for her either, I felt

85

less incompetent. Like a flock of birds synchronizing its movements in some unspoken fashion, we swayed our steering in response to the slightest deviation in the crowd. The forty-minute ride was extremely nerve wracking and I swore I would never go out on a bike again. I forgot this was Beijing's rush hour, not normal commerce. Perhaps if I had known this was to be the first and last time I was to mount my bike in the summer of 1989 outside the walls of the compound, I would have exhibited more tolerance for the Zen of bicycle riding, interpreting it in a more positive light.

    I had forgotten about the joy biking could bring. Last year, before our flight to the United States, I wanted to do something to say good-bye to the city that had changed my soul. I wanted to create a personal ritual. I jumped on my bike and decided to take one symbolic final ride in all the four directions. Past piles of giant cabbages and shiny eggplants, stands of expensive bananas and succulent oranges, I first pedalled east. The neighborhood men in undershirts, smoking cheap cigarettes and playing pool on the street, motioned for me to join them. Since I couldn't speak Chinese and I didn't know how to play pool, I smiled generously and, shaking my head from side to side, turned north.

    Past highway ramps and concrete overpasses, I contentedly drifted down the cool tree-lined boulevard that led to the opulent hotels reserved for foreigners. Earlier that evening, a friend and I had dined on giant prawns and dainty cakes in the expensive revolving restaurant of the Great Wall Sheraton. Reaching that hotel, I turned back and retraced my route past the Kun

Friendship

Lun Hotel disco until I came to the street where our hotel was situated.

Heading west, I passed the Japanese-American Friendship Hospital where patients sauntered on the grounds in blue and white "prison pajamas" as I called them. Just a few weeks before, I had entertained the Department of Dentistry there with my mouthful of large white teeth. I wanted to have them looked at because I thought plaque might be building up from drinking so much Coca Cola on the scorching summer days. Everybody in the office was invited to peer into my perfectly maintained mouth. They laughed and wanted to know why I had come in. Finally, one doctor asked when I had last seen a dentist. When I told him six weeks ago, he told me nothing could be wrong. People should go to the dentist every few years, he instructed, as he placated me by trying out his new ultrasound device on my teeth.

I continued past my hotel where the street turned into a pot-holed dirt road, strewn with horse manure and scarred by ruts filled with stagnant water. Riding down the bumpy road I passed horse-drawn carts and verdant vegetable patches. I stopped just as the sun was setting at the end of the road I was exploring.

Heading south, my final direction, I found myself riding parallel to the canal, the first place I had gone for a walk with Jake and the Chinese director of the program on my first day in China. No longer disgusted by the sight and smell of human waste floating in its waters, I rode along the embankment while families, children, and lovers looked at my ecstatic face. I gazed up at an

Beijing: The New Forbidden City

umbrella of cottony, cumulus clouds in the fading blue sky where stars were just starting to peek out. I silently thanked the heavens for protecting me and allaying my fears of the unknown.

That evening, I was both sad and elated at the prospect of leaving China. I took comfort from the sky, knowing that the same blanket would cover me wherever I go and China would always be with me. Turning around, I raced as fast as my legs could take me, blaming the tears joyfully washing down my face on the wind.

FABLE

JUNE 2

Beijing: The New Forbidden City

The second day of June was a very special day for us, partly because the of date, partly because of the many jubilant experiences we crammed into it. We began the day in our comfortable little van, on our way to the Qi Gong Institute. Somehow our conversation turned to the meanings derived from the sounds of our names in Chinese, and our host enthusiastically accepted the royal task of crowning us with new names.

"Dairne" in Chinese sounded like "enemy." Because her name was the antithesis of her relationship to the group and the translator in particular, he decided to construe her name as "friend." "Martha" evoked the image of "ma," a horse, but more poetically, "a horse beneath the trees rustled by the wind." My roommate "Anna" sounded like "a safe place" and this was certainly the way I came to feel about her when she would reach out to comfort me during the unending nights spliced with gunfire commencing with the massacre . "Lynsay," my colleague and assistant leader, conjured up the picture of a "forest"; to me, a pine forest, pure, eternal, and stately. His composure and presence were some of the very reasons I had hand-picked him to lead the group.

Fable

"Stan" sounded like "never tired," descriptive of his enthusiasm for study as well as his tireless devotion to his wife Gigi who was not in our training program but had accompanied Stan for her own share of adventure. Our translator's name meant "ocean," and to us he was a sea of tranquility. My name continued to be equated with its closest equivalent, "sky," not based upon how it sounded but because Jake had translated it for me the year before.

Last but not least was Robert, always attentive and polite. Playfully we probed, "What does Robert mean?" Our guide thoughtfully searched for the words within his finite English vocabulary to accurately describe Robert. When he delightfully announced "turnip," we burst out laughing and repeated, "Turnip? Turnip?" as if we could not have heard him right. Who would want their name to mean turnip? Could only a mother love a turnip? By this time we were comfortable enough with each other to take the license to poke fun. Somehow the name did seem fitting. Robert was like a solid, hearty vegetable, as firmly rooted in the earth as he was by our side.

Each name became a revelation, contributing to the unique image of our group energy. We were "the friend," "the one who never tired," "a turnip," and "the wind blowing through the trees with a horse nearby," " set against the backdrop of "the forest," "the ocean," "the sky," and "a safe place." It was such a picturesque moment that I vowed to create an oil painting and make it into a Christmas card someday so as not to forget the members of our unique entourage.

That night, before I went to sleep, I sat in my bed beneath the dim night light and wrote the following story:

> There was a man who lived by a forest and an ocean. The smell of the pine carried by the sea often made him long for things he didn't have. So, sometimes, during the day, even though he was never tired in his simple life, he would lie down on the ground coated with pine needles and look up at the expansive blue sky. The wind rustled through the leaves of the tree above his head and his nearby horse gently neighed. After thinking of many things, his good friend brought him a turnip for lunch and he felt very safe. And life was good.

This clever little fable seemed to tie our beings up in an interwoven net. Sometime later, during the night of the slaughter, we asked each other why we had been thrown together to experience all of this. Of course numerous connections unveiled themselves, but I kept thinking of this fable. On the flight home to America, like a child who needed a bedtime story in order to dream, my little tale whispered in my mind as I drifted in and out of a fitful sleep. Only later did the meaning of the story become clear to me: The turnip was democracy!

FRIVOLITY

Beijing: The New Forbidden City

The second day of June was also Dairne's birthday. In keeping with the spirit of "friend," she generously treated us all to a dinner celebration in her honor. That evening we were also scheduled to go see the acrobats, the first in a string of evening entertainments provided by the academy. It turned out to be the last.

We started our dinner with a mouth-watering Szechuan chicken smothered with hot sauce and peanuts, one of our favorite dishes, along with a variety of vegetables, hard-to-find fried potatoes, rice, and the inevitable beer or Coke that complemented every meal but breakfast. We could have stayed all evening, laughing, eating, drinking, and joking, but since we didn't want to miss out on the acrobats, we opted to resume our frivolity later that evening.

The Beijing acrobats were a delight. From act to act, we laughed so hard at their agility and absurdities that tears streamed down our faces. Applauding, we smiled at each other, needing no words to convey the unanimity of our pleasure. From card tricks to juggling acts, the entire performance was colored with dramatic costumes and makeup. The children in the audience could only sigh in admiration. As I studied the young

Frivolity

children and middle-aged actors performing their crafts with pride, I compared how different and presumably more enjoyable their lives were than the lives of the adolescent youths I had seen carrying heavy cauldrons, stoves, food, and utensils to street corners where they cooked every evening for the hungry populace looking for local specialties. Biking behind them as they trudged on foot, their young backs looked as if they could only house broken hearts, and I was thankful my three brothers had been "lucky" enough to have been spared heavy labor. This evening, life in Communist China seemed somewhat less than equitably equal.

After the performance, we resumed our celebration. Our bus driver left us off at the familiar junction where we had purchased our bicycles, which also happened to have the ice cream stand closest to our lodging. We all decided to get cones of delicious ice milk to go along with the cake we were keeping hidden from Dairne. Chinese ice cream is good, not cloyingly rich but clean and refreshing, and some of the students couldn't resist treating themselves to more than one of the twenty-five-cent sundries.

Robert had planned ahead of time to have two cones. He returned to join the group with one in each hand. Just as he went to lick his first frozen mound, he knocked the coveted scoop to the ground. We giggled a bit before we noticed that he wasn't too happy about our reaction. Shrugging his shoulders, he started to attack the other one when the exact same thing happened. Unable to restrain ourselves any longer, we laughed at

Beijing: The New Forbidden City

the repetition of events, even though Robert was obviously displeased. Determined to have his ice cream, one vanilla and one chocolate, he started complaining about how he had already spent two *renminbi* on ice cream. When someone reminded him that this was less than fifty cents, he good-naturedly joined in the levity with us, in typical "turnip" fashion.

Standing at the busy junction teaming with Friday evening nightlife, I pulled a small, slightly crushed cake from my backpack. While Dairne wasn't looking, we nestled self-igniting candles on top of the sugary confection. Bicyclists and pedestrians stopped to watch the group of barbarians singing "Happy Birthday" and acting as if they were mentally deranged, such was our lack of inhibition. But what unquestionably must have boggled their minds the most were those indestructible candles, lighting up time after time even after they had been blown out.

By 9:00 P.M., we were tired. We had to get up early the next morning to go to the hospital, plus I had promised the students a major shopping spree and lunch at the Jianguo Hotel.

We sauntered back to our rooms passing a sawdust-strewn sidewalk where carpenters worked by the beam of a flashlight making furniture on the street. We had been in China one exhilarating week. Tomorrow we hoped to spring free from our daily routine and reward ourselves with the richness of new cultural experiences. It was the evening before the Tiananmen massacre.

*FRENCH FRIES
AND
FALLEN DRAGONS
JUNE 3*

Beijing: The New Forbidden City

Something was amiss but I couldn't put my finger on it. The doctor with whom we had been studying for a week was not her usual composed self; she seemed distracted, tired, and almost inattentive to us and her patients. People kept dropping by the hospital to talk to her covertly. We could only assume what all the activity was about, but it appeared to be upsetting our mentor.

By the end of the morning, we had completed six days of internship which meant our schedules would rotate the following week. When I thanked our doctor for giving us the opportunity to study with her, I was surprised by her show of emotions when she tenderly embraced me, crooning, "Sky, Sky." I responded, "*Jiejie*, sister," always anxious to try out my new vocabulary. In response, she cried, "I can't bear to separate myself from you!" Still holding her, I pulled away slightly to look into her eyes. Her outburst seemed unusually strong given that next week we would only be going to the adjacent room to study with another doctor. I could only surmise she was particularly sentimental that day.

"*Mingnian, mingnian*, next year, next year," I promised, reminding her that I would return to study with her. In retrospect, I think she knew something

French Fries and Fallen Dragons

irrevocable was about to happen and that we might never see each other again.

I dashed down the stairs of the hospital to meet the students who were ready for another grand day. They weren't sure at first what they wanted to do, but I managed to convince them they shouldn't pass up a chance for another shopping spree with me. After a change of clothes, we descended upon the Jianguo Hotel for chewy hamburgers, frigid Cokes, and simulated french fries. The restaurant was having a promotion of "American food" displayed on a special placemat that depicted the varieties of hamburgers Americans supposedly ate. The four of us from Santa Fe wondered what a New Mexico hamburger would be like as we ordered the concoction. It came smothered with barbecue sauce instead of the authentic green chili and gooey melted cheese we were used to eating in our home state. Quite honestly, the hamburgers were awful, but we were entertained just seeing how the entrees were prepared.

One of the students purchased an American newspaper. I immediately asked to look at it, and dove into the commentary on China in an attempt to find out what was going on. The editorial did not sound positive: It clearly stated the predicament with the students was intolerable and the hard-liners would prevail. I also learned Zhao Zi Yang had offered to resign, but his resignation was deferred so he could be criticized, a ploy designed to discourage popular opinion from swinging in his philosophical direction. Smirking at the distasteful news, I swallowed a last mouthful of bitter coffee sickeningly sweetened with condensed milk, before I folded up the newspaper and put it in my bag, planning to study more later.

We spent the better part of the afternoon shopping at the bazaar next to the Jianguo Hotel. The first stall I stopped at was one of my favorites, a cluttered antique stand filled with colorful silk wedding skirts, delicately carved miniature snuff bottles, embroidered slippers that once encased bound feet, and every variety of porcelain imaginable. A milk-white and Nanking-blue teapot in the shape of a dragon caught my eye. No sooner had I picked it up to contemplate its purchase than I clumsily dropped it to the floor. Frowning and muttering, the stern proprietress gathered the remnants and began gluing the broken pieces together. We could not find one small fragment missing from the lid. Grimly I thought I would have to purchase the pot, so I inquired how much it would cost. When the vendor replied "Sixty yuan," I counter-offered, "How about fifty?" Graciously, she acquiesced. Resolving to be more careful, I cautiously stowed the delicate teapot in my knapsack while I pondered why the dragon's back had to break.

Shopping was particularly good that Saturday, and the students' search for silk shirts and bathrobes, cotton tee-shirts, tablecloths, and baby clothes was fruitful. After leaving the bazaar, we decided to get some exercise and walk the block to the Friendship Store for another cold drink and more earnest shopping. On the way, we encountered two students selling buttons with the international peace symbol and the word *Victor* emblazoned upon them. We went crazy over the pins. Although we would have paid anything to possess them,

French Fries and Fallen Dragons

I was in the habit of bartering the asking price down, so I offered less. The Chinese students finally conceded to my offer, commenting that I was "very clever." They added, "It is a very good day to go to Tiananmen Square," but earlier that day our host and a doctor had cautioned us to stay away, the first time they had ever done so. Their respected advice, plus our own instincts, saved us from the violence that occurred later on that grisly morning.

FEVOR

JUNE 3

Beijing: The New Forbidden City

We secured our prize possessions to our backpacks, keeping them visible so we could boastfully flaunt them in the three-tiered Friendship Store which catered exclusively to foreigners. I made my way from counter to counter, stocked with both domestic and imported goods, looking for gifts for children back home and cultural artifacts for myself. At the foot of the escalator, a new display of soft-washed denim Levi's caused me to reflect on my visit to the same store the previous year. I also noticed that the makeup department had expanded; it now featured expensive Christian Dior lipsticks, albeit in discontinued colors. I marvelled at the change one year could make and how encroaching Westernization had invaded a store off-limits to native Chinese.

Hours of relentless shopping in the naked sun had temporarily sapped our energy, so we decided to take a taxi to the Beijing Hotel. A fleet hovered outside the Friendship Store but all of the drivers refused to take us anywhere. We couldn't understand what was going on. Deciphering gesticulations, we guessed that traffic was congested in the direction of the Beijing Hotel and Tiananmen Square; no one could go that way, or else no one wanted to.

Fevor

Buses were also abandoned along Chang'an Avenue. Without the services of an interpreter, we were unable to ascertain the reason for this strange occurrence. As we debated over what to do, two poor workers pedalling flatbed wooden carts offered to take us to our destination. Compared with both bus and taxi fares, their rates were exorbitant, but we were lazy and relatively affluent, so we arranged to ride in the two vehicles. We hopped on, three to a cart, and the skinny young men who must have weighed less than any one of us towed our group down the three long blocks to the Beijing Hotel.

Although we laughed over how much fun it was, we felt embarrassed that in the twentieth century we were being conspicuously hauled by human effort along the main street of downtown Beijing. I reflected on the euphoric feeling I had experienced the previous year when a friend and I hired a pedicab driver to transport us from the Beijing Hotel to the domicile where we were living in the northwest quadrant of the city. Under a Prussian blue sky strung with crystal stars, we were leisurely escorted through the sultry night down the major avenues abounding with street life. When our pale hair caught the gleam of street lights that illuminated the enchanting evening, we heard the familiar "Change money, change money." That evening, under the eastern constellations, it seemed we were perceived more as economic entities than as women alone in the night. As it turned out, no sexual allusions or flirtatious behavior ever characterized our interaction with Chinese men during our visit, with the exception of one night when a taxi driver invited my roommate to go on a ride with him

Beijing: The New Forbidden City

to the Great Wall!

Riding at a fairly brisk pace, bedecked with victory buttons, we felt like heroes galloping into the city. A driver pedalling parallel to our cart began to openly discuss politics with us. He named American Presidents and then would add, *hen hao* (very good) or *bu hao* (bad) after their names. "President Kennedy, *hen hao*. President Nixon, *bu hao*. President Reagan, *bu hao*. President Bush, *hen hao*, " he recited like a dutiful student. When we named the Chinese heads of state, he supplied the judgement. "Zhao Zi Yang?" "*Hen hao.*" "Li Peng?" "*Bu hao.* "

With the mention of Deng Xiaoping, an angry snarl crossed his otherwise beaming face and he pantomimed shooting. Shocked by the strength of the feelings that must have caused his sentiments to surface so blatantly, we shook our heads discouragingly to show that we did not think this was the solution to China's internal problems. Like the students on the square, we too wanted to believe that somehow a nonviolent resolution, a peaceful transition, was possible.

Forming our fingers into peace signs, taking pictures, and talking politics between the carts, we were deliriously happy. Our ride ended at the foot of Wanfujing where we planned to continue shopping. In the next few hours, we browsed through the three-story Beijing Arts and Crafts Store, the Foreign Language Bookstore, the Beijing Department Store, an acupuncture supply and herb store, a grocery market, and my favorite antique store. While perusing amidst the Cerrilian blue kingfisher jewelry, vintage clothing from imperial days, heirloom jade, and handsomely crafted bronze, I fondly recalled my treasured watercolor of the Summer Palace bought there the year before as a momento of that magnificent summer. Then, for what would be the last time, we reconvened in the lounge of the Beijing Hotel to make plans for the evening and compare purchases over refreshments. We noted that the hotel was conspicuously empty for this time of night and that we were the only Americans in the lobby. Exhausted by the day's excursion, we decided to postpone dancing at the Holiday Inn until the following Saturday. Most of the students planned to retreat to the dorm, but Lynsay and I thought we'd walk up Wanfujing one more time to look for an unobtrusive medical supply house which we were told could be found just outside the retail district.

Most stores were closing and the streets were uncommonly deserted. The alley we were looking for kept eluding us and, before we knew it, we had meandered around to the Palace Hotel located about halfway back to our residence. We decided to go inside and gaze at the items in the expensive gift store. The hotel's opulence, with its massive marble accommodations, overwhelmed us in contrast to the poverty we had just left in the post-war neighborhood. In my sneakers and jeans, I suddenly felt out of place.

We decided to grab a taxi. After the driver dropped us off on a narrow street close to the dorm, we passed by our favorite local restaurant where we saw the students who had left us earlier. We joined them in their meal, nibbling on peanuts and bits of fried rice, happily

Beijing: The New Forbidden City

allowing ourselves to be pampered by the smiling young woman and her husband who operated the small eatery. That evening we were free to enjoy our personal time as we wished, so everyone went their separate ways. Tomorrow promised to be another hectic day of sight-seeing and shopping, so I decided to spend a quiet evening by myself to regain my energy. I unwound in a long hot bubble bath and gave myself a facial to remove the accumulated grit of city life. Renewed, I decided to take care of a traveller's domestic chores: stow my purchases in a suitcase, organize my outfits for the next week, and rinse out my hand washables. I concluded the day by writing in my travel diary, enjoying the peace and comfort of the little room which had become my sanctuary.

Just as I was about to go to bed, students started to tumble into my room, two-by-two, describing what they had done that evening. Dairne and Robert had the most exciting story to tell. On their private venture, they had gone off on a short bike ride down Dongzhimennei towards the freeway, until they were stopped by a barricade of buses obstructing the overpass. Their story of the carnival-like atmosphere on the streets held us spellbound. I couldn't imagine parents, grandparents, children, and babies in their pajamas roaming the streets past bedtime. Although Dairne and Robert were unable understand a word of the incessant chatter surrounding them, there was no doubt in their minds that it was connected to the energy generated by the student movement.

Fevor

Once they were recognized as Americans, Dairne and Robert were pushed to the side of a bus where young adults hung out of windows and stood on top of the vehicle cheering. The crowd clamored for our friends to climb up onto the roof of the bus. Fear welled up in them as the will of the crowd became clear, but it was easier to go with the desire of the mob rather than resist, so they allowed themselves to be hoisted up onto the bus. There they were adulated like heroes on this night they would never forget.

As Dairne and Robert unraveled their incredible tale, we felt as caught up in the thrill as they had been. I suggested, "Let's go to the square now," for I had heard the early hours of the morning were the time when the students discussed their politics and strategies. But Dairne cautioned, " No, no, not tonight. The streets are wild. This night belongs to the Chinese people." Listening to her common sense and considering the late hour, we decided to stay put, a decision that may have shaped the rest of our lives.

FOURTH OF JUNE

Beijing: The New Forbidden City

I awoke about midnight drenched in sweat from a nightmare. I had dreamed that the city was ravaged by war and there was no way out. Amidst the rubble, I searched for a telephone to call home. Although we were all safe in the dream, it was clear that we would never be able to leave the city.

Recovering from the horrifying nightmare, I thought I could hear whispering outside my bedroom window. I had never heard voices after I had gone to bed, so this behavior seemed noteworthy. I stood by the window and strained to see if I could see anyone. Maybe this was when the Chinese people discussed politics, shrouded by the anonymity of the night?

On my first trip to China, I had been sure that there was an unspoken consensus, a common agreement amongst the people, to make personal sacrifices, if necessary, for the common good. But now the student unrest was upsetting my neat story of life in China and I couldn't help but wonder when and where people talked about their dreams. Perhaps tonight, under the stars, a midnight soiree was underway.

I dozed off again only to be awakened by a huge bang at 12:20 A.M. There was little doubt in my mind that it was the sound of gunfire, even though I had never heard gunfire before. Could it be? Was a crackdown underway? My heart hung like a hummingbird suspended over a fragile flower. I didn't hear another thing but I was unable to fall back asleep. I stayed awake until, after another twenty minutes, the identical sound repeated itself. Aha - I had not imagined it! I knew in my heart, frozen with fear, that the square was being cleared.

Standing by my bedroom window, I noted the congregation of whispers had been replaced by a deafening hush. No lights illuminated the windows. A little later, I heard the same thunderous roar, a sound one might imagine coming from firepower about three miles away which was the distance from our shelter to Tiananmen Square. Throwing my face into my hands, I began to moan: "Why are they killing their own children? Why are there no screams of anguish from others like me who must have heard the gunfire? Why do horrifying acts always come under the cover of night?" My body shook as I grieved out loud for China, saying, "This will be the saddest day in Chinese history."

Needing to spill my grief, I ran to Martha and Dairne's room next to mine and pounded on the door. They arose sleepily and opened the portal. "They're killing them, they're killing the students! Listen to the guns!" I narrated breathlessly. "What? No! Who? It can't be! What guns?" they echoed, as I paced back and forth in their room clutching my chest. By this time there were no more intervals between the shots. Now the penetrating whine of ambulances added to the cacophony. It did not take long for Martha and Dairne's incredulity to dissolve once I tuned their ears to the onrush of sounds.

Lynsay and Robert could hear nothing from their quarters where an air conditioner's mechanical moan blocked out the sounds of the night. When I awakened them, they came out into the corridor and stood with us. Shocked, they tried to rationalize the incessant popping of guns that seemed even closer now: "Perhaps it's flares, or blanks, or crowd dispersers?" Lynsay proposed, but I could see in his eyes he believed otherwise and he was only trying to pacify the group. Anna soon joined our small group. Still in disbelief ourselves, we filled her in.

Stan and Gigi sleeping in the room on the other side of mine never stirred. Their apartment, also equipped with an air conditioner, insulated them from the evil of the night. Protectively, we refrained from awaking them; Gigi had been very ill since we had arrived in China and we wanted her to rest. We realized that, in all likelihood, the next few days would be grueling enough and she would be doubly taxed because of her health.

Pacing the corridor, we peered out of the windows, even though the only view they offered was the brick building next to ours. Lynsay later told us he could hear bullets ricocheting off of the dorm. As it started to get lighter, we heard some voices in the courtyard below. Paralyzed by confusion and fear, we didn't know what to do, but we felt compelled to do something. Some of the students went out to the courtyard to wander about in their night clothes. Beneath the street lights, they looked like friendly ghosts. I went with some others over to the academy to see if anyone there knew what was going on.

Fourth of June

Outside the academy, we ran into Brian, a visiting chiropractor and Beijing expert, who had been out late that Saturday night. When we told him what we had heard, he said he had been down to the square earlier that evening but hadn't seen anything. Upstairs, we encountered a young Chinese man who was friendly with the students. In a restrained and feeble voice, he confirmed, "Yes, there has been fighting. The government is ending the student occupation. Ambulances are making their way to the square and they are full of soldiers, not medical personnel.

"Students have been killed; I think about four," he went on. "The students wanted too much too fast. I tried to tell them. We all tried to tell them that things wouldn't change as fast as they demanded. But we joined in because they are our last hope."

"What did they want?" we asked.

"Freedom of speech, freedom of the press, freedom to congregate, corruption reduced in the bureaucracy," he flatly replied.

We met back in my bedroom like a grown-up pajama party without any mirth. Martha, Dairne, and Anna made tea for everyone and shared their cherished cookies and candy bars to help nourish our systems and subdue the shock. By 2:30 A.M., the gunfire had reached it zenith and the streets surrounding us were flooded with people. Like an ocean, the cries of thousands of citizens blended into a bleating roar. Interjected with machine gun fire, "Ahhh, Ahhh, Ahhh..." was all we could hear. The faces of 10,000 people folded into my soul. Helplessly, we huddled in the dark, trying to keep up our strength as our imaginations filled in the missing pictures to explain the enclosing dirge.

As dawn approached, we began began discussing democracy, freedom, and how China would change if it could ever become free. Why couldn't it become free? What historical shackle crippled it? We tried to figure out why we were in China at this moment and why we were with each other. What should we do? What was going to become of us? We feared not so much for our own lives as for the lives of our Chinese friends who were activists, and for the future of China which now seemed as unalterably ordained as its past.

Would the small ruling elite ever abdicate its addictive hold on China's burgeoning population of over one billion people? The Great Wall and the Forbidden City were not obsolete artifacts surviving Imperial China solely for sightseers to visit. Nor were they stagnant symbols of the feudal past. Rather, they had come to serve as futile boundaries of experience within which the most populous nation on earth was forced to live.

By 5:00 A.M., most of my friends had drifted back to their own bedrooms seeking solitude. The night of terror was almost over and only sporadic gunfire spread through the smoky sky. Good and evil had collided outside our bedroom windows and on the Square of Heavenly Peace. I thought, "This madness wrought by self-importance and might does not make right."

FIRE AND RAIN

JUNE 4

Beijing: The New Forbidden City

Shopping for silk, dabbling in delicacies, seeking serenity in the Llama Temple — these were our plans for that fateful Sunday. We had hoped to mix what we considered to be a proper amount of consumerism with a little decadence and a good strong dose of the search for meaning. It was to be the first weekend excursion where we would be able to play the tourist role, relax, and contemplate another face of China.

For the Chinese, Sundays are ordinarily the only day off from a long six-day work week. After household chores are completed, they spend their time sipping homemade sodas, window shopping with the family along Wanfujing, or strolling in one of the many parks interspersed throughout urban Beijing.

But this Sunday, the entire nation remained stunned in the aftermath of the interminable night stalked by terror, punctuated by death. It was the first morning in the wake of the Tiananmen massacre.

At 5:30 that morning, my roommate and I consoled each other one last time, and finally started to drift off to sleep. Random gunfire reverberated over the symphony of birds that normally announces the arriving day. My heart fluttered wildly, speeding up so fast I

Fire and Rain

thought it would burst from my chest, slowing down so dramatically that I was sure it would stop. Finally, worn out, I fell into a short sleep. One hour later it was time to get up.

The previous night we had made plans to convene in the morning to find out what had actually happened and plan what was to transpire next. Even though I desperately required rest, I got up with my alarm, bathed and dressed in a trance-like state. No coordinated outfit for me today, I thought, as I pulled on the identical jeans and tee-shirt I had worn the night before when we had wandered through the compound like sleep walkers, trying to gather information on what was happening.

Some of the students seeking news had ventured onto the streets early that morning only to witness soldiers carting battered, bullet-ridden bodies through the lanes diverging off Dongzhimennei. Our head translator arrived outside our dormitory slightly tardy and breathless after pedaling from his home on the other side of town. He wanted to make sure we were alright. Visibly shaken, wane, and unusually emotional, he reported, "Things are very, very bad. Many students have gone to heaven. The hearts of the Chinese people are filled with tears." We all tried to restrain our emotions and find our obstructed voices to scrape together a picture of what had befallen the city already beloved to us.

Our translator confirmed an attack had been ordered by Deng Xiaoping and Li Peng and said that now everyone in the city was afraid. The grief and heaviness of his heart had not diminished his sense of responsibility or his concern for us. We assured him that we would all stay put for the day, like most people in the city, so that he could return to his apartment and his wife. As if needing permission to leave, he repeatedly asked for our promises that we would stay within the safe orbit of the compound.

Exhausted and stricken with grief, we were left to deal with the horror in our own way. All I could think of was getting details that could help us understand China's predicament to share with the group, so I headed over to the academy to sit in the student lounge, watch Chinese television, and speak to anyone who came my way.

The day was ghostly grey and cold with cloud-cloaked skies. Its feeling seemed to match the oppression that weighed upon us. I had always felt nature could not help but be affected by man's actions; a clear sunny day would have too seriously juxtaposed our sentiments with the energy emanating from overhead. Soon the grayness generated a bitter rain accompanied by threatening thunder and lashes of lightning, a torrent pounding so hard it crackled and sizzled like fire. I recalled the words of a theology teacher I once had who believed nature would participate in man's redemption because man was the conscience of nature. I had never fully realized what she meant until that day when the weather seemed mandated to mirror the grief and outrage of a powerless people.

We spent hours trying to construct some sense out of what we could only picture in our minds. Reports ranged that fifty to three hundred to several thousand had been killed in the city, but most estimates were in the conservative range. As we shared stories of the night, thoughtful school maintenance attendants brought thermoses of steaming water for tea to the lounge where everyone had congregated. Comforting ourselves, we reflectively sipped the weak jasmine tea I steeped. Ritual took on new significance in a world which had become unpredictable overnight.

FIRESIDE CHATS

Beijing: The New Forbidden City

One of our German friends left the compound alone to go down to the Beijing Hotel and pick up some film being developed there. We were all very worried about her and condemned her rash behavior—venturing out as if it had been an ordinary day! She returned from the city hours later, ashen from the scenes she had witnessed.

Uneventfully, Ursula had biked to the Beijing Hotel, determined to pick up her film in case the government chose to evacuate foreigners. As we might have predicted, she found the film counter closed, the hotel defaced and deserted. Since she was downtown, she decided to pedal to Tiananmen Square in an attempt to verify the consequences of the night of wrath. The streets of the city, normally so organized, were in utter disarray. Smoldering buses, parked every which way, emitted thick greasy black smoke into the morning air still dense with odors of the night's gunfire. When she reached the square, off-limits now to curious passers-by, she found it tattered with paralyzed tanks, broken concrete, and smashed fences. Ursula thought she could see piles of inert bodies in the crippled buses burning on the square.

Fireside Chats

After Ursula completed her alarming story, Gilbert, one of the students living in our dormitory who had a shortwave radio, invited us into his room to listen to the British Broadcasting Corporation (BBC) broadcast. We anxiously awaited the afternoon news report to see if the world outside the Great Wall had heard of the night's atrocities and to hear their analyses of the circumstances. Never before had a radio been so important.

We had already gathered some information from watching television. Chinese broadcasts denied that anything had happened other than, "Bad people threw rocks and stones at the tanks. One soldier was killed. The troops showed great restraint." The German, American, Swiss, and Brazilian embassies all reported that many people had been killed or wounded. According to their news segments, soldiers disguised in plain clothes had been making their way into the Forbidden City and the People's Mansion all week long, while we naively studied in the hospitals and played on the streets. From these locations, troops streamed out onto the square during the massacre after reportedly undergoing drugging and brainwashing to kill.

The "Voice of Freedom" segment of the BBC news report quivered and broke as the announcer reported that a massacre of substantial proportion had occurred in China. According to this announcer, the crowd had been told they would be killed if they didn't leave the square. Then tanks had smashed down the small iron fences bordering the square and begun rolling over students. Estimates were that one to two hundred students were killed and about a thousand were wounded.

It was almost impossible to accurately determine how many had been murdered, he said, but the city's hospitals were overflowing. Government troops were already assiduously scrubbing blood from the square, which they claimed had been defaced by students. The British newscaster replayed a recording of one of their correspondents who was at the square, crying out as he ran for his life while people of every age—children, babies, grandparents, and students—fell to the ground around him.

We were all silent as we huddled on two twin beds and the floor, trying to decipher the report through the heavy static on the airways. The radio became our lifesaver, a flame of freedom, our connection with the outside world, the vigilant monitor of what was happening around us, and the social conscience of people all over the planet decrying the slaughter of innocent, armless people. We clung to every word as if our lives depended upon it.

The British government declared, "Anyone who goes out is foolhardy and is committing an extraordinary act of defiance," in response to the curfew that had been ordered between 3:00 and 6:00 P.M. Helicopters whirled close overhead, like giant poisonous insects, reminding us of the government's venomous sting. Whoever thought we, children born in the land of the free, would be listening to the exploits of brave Chinese students through the eyes of the British via a shortwave radio broadcast? We waited suspended on an island of suppression.

We all agreed that the anguish we felt, though oppressive, could not be compared with the agony the

Chinese people were suffering when members of their families did not return with the dawn. While we said we were not afraid, our hearts were wild and greatly saddened by the act that in one fell swoop threw China back to its feudal past. As one Chinese friend dejectedly summarized, "China has made one step forward and six backward."

FACADE

JUNE 5

By the end of the day, the Canadian and Italian students studying at our school had been rescued by their embassies. Everyone remaining at the compound was exhausted, so we tried to get some sleep while waiting to find out more about the state of the political situation. Although we knew our personal safety was not at stake, we were deeply disturbed by the turn the government had taken.

The city remained calm overnight. In the morning, one of the Chinese doctors told us that the "peaceful" climate indicated the citizens were afraid because they knew they could be killed. Our translator, who showed up for morning clinic even though it was cancelled, told us, "Beijing University was attacked by soldiers. When people congregate in groups, they are shot at."

On top of all of this, we ran into Gigi, on her way back from breakfast looking deathly pale and weakened. Seeing that she needed medical attention, we approached the director of the school who agreed she should go to a hospital. Our faithful bus driver, who was an activist in the pro-democracy movement, refused at first to take the director, Gigi, and Stan to the dangerous belt of the city where the hospital for foreigners was located, fearing not for his own safety but for theirs. Thanks to the indomitable will of the director, he was soon convinced of the emergency situation and the threesome was transported to the hospital. Hours later, we heard that tests showed Gigi was so anemic she needed a transfusion and that she would be staying overnight with Stan by her side. The director returned safely after making sure Gigi was well taken care of. Now she became even more revered by the students for her bravery and persistence.

    Since we were barred from the training hospital, the director set up a class for us on campus. I was sure the ward we had been studying in, like most, had been converted into emergency facilities for the wounded and a morgue for the dead. Vociferously, we protested that we didn't expect anyone to teach us under these conditions; not only were we in no shape to learn, even more so, we did not want our doctors to pretend our classes could have any meaning in comparison with the life and death situations lurking outside the academy. But we were defeated. As we were to witness on more than one occasion, the Chinese sense of responsibility remained undaunted even in the face of personal tragedy.

    Perhaps it was for the best, as the class helped structure our time which was becoming so warped by the desperate acts of dying men. Some of us attended; others rested and tried to recover from the shock of the last few days. The lecturer explained the lesson perfectly in her demure little voice, as did the translator, although tears drifted like clouds into their eyes and ours when we let our minds wander. Like automatons, we took notes, asked questions, and somehow survived the morning.

Although no one had any appetite, we convened in the cafeteria to share news, talk to the other students at the academy, and keep up our strength. Sitting at my table was Ursula, the German dentist, Celia, a student from Brazil, and a Chinese girl who spoke English. My head whirled amidst translations of stories told in three languages.

We were tired and depressed and our rooms were disheveled, but I was grateful that we were at the academy, relatively in touch with the world and amongst friends, instead of at an isolated hotel like we were the year before. I thought back on the best friend I had made in China on my previous journey, and how she had claimed that she was never depressed, regardless of our attempts to convince her that surely she had. I wondered if, wherever she was, she now knew the meaning of the word.

We had food, water, classes, radio, television, books, Coca-Cola, chocolate, and space to exercise. Still none of it soothed our broken hearts. What could be worse than being shanghaied in Beijing?

FRIEND OR FOE

JUNE 6

Beijing: The New Forbidden City

*L*ike the proverbial calm before the storm, Monday was virtually dead, but that evening, under the shroud of darkness, the guns returned. The next morning our translator, in his characteristic manner, told us not to worry: Rumor had it that an assassination attempt had been made on Li Peng's life. Even though it had been unsuccessful, the attack indicated that the people would no longer stand for the heinous crimes carried out under the command of Deng Xiaoping and his cohorts. Word was circulating that a "good army" was on its way to rescue Beijing from the murderous jaws of the government.

Our translator also informed us that the soldiers who were tired from the skirmish on the square and policing the streets would not be able to hold out for long. Even though citizens were unarmed, they had found a way to retaliate by not bringing food and water to the soldiers. Soon the People's Liberation Army, the traitors, would be defeated. We looked at each other in disbelief. Could he really be this naive? Were the people so innocent that they didn't realize they would be killed immediately if they disobeyed the orders of the soldiers?

Friend or Foe

We attended class again that morning. It was no easier but we all went through the motions anyway. At least we were able to get the teachers to cancel afternoon classes by refusing to attend.

Our translator returned after his lunch on the street to report that he had seen a baby and his father gunned down when the infant gurgled while they were waiting in a line to buy bread. "The soldiers must be drugged," he rationalized; this was the only explanation he could imagine for what he had witnessed. The din of daily commerce, which was just beginning to resume in the city, plus the smoke screen of sunshine effectively sequestered us from the world outside the academy that day, a world we hadn't seen since Saturday. But it could not protect our souls from the chaos closing in around us.

At three o'clock, curfew was imposed again and there was talk of a food shortage. The campus went berserk. Doctors, workers, and families living within the academy's compound swarmed like hornets towards the small convenience store on the premises that sold a few food staples and personal hygiene products. We too followed the crowd into the tiny store, anticipating that the compound cafeteria might run out of food. Within the store, customers scrambled frantically, reaching for crackers and instant noodle soups. Shoppers exited with piles of enough cellophane packages to feed their families for a few days. Waiting our turn, we purchased soup, crackers, cookies, and soda, just in case we needed a stockpile of food. I had never seen such Pandemonium; it looked as if we were not the only ones expecting a period of confinement to the compound. As I watched the

145

mayhem, I decided it was time to leave the country. After all, we might not have another chance! I needed to talk to the group.

I decided to call an emergency meeting to discuss our options. After hearing the story of what had happened to the father and his baby at noon in broad daylight, I was certain the city was still out of control and unpredictable. Where was all this leading? What was building up? Would the Chinese people tolerate even the pointless shooting of little children? Did they have any choice? Without weapons, how could they overthrow the decaying regime which was strangling life at every opportunity? Could freedom only be purchased with more bloodshed? What was the solution?

Talk of civil war was underway. Supposedly, troops from the north, the "good soldiers," were on their way to Beijing to battle Deng's special cadre of soldiers who had fought in Vietnam. Reportedly, Deng's troops had been brought in from the south and therefore did not feel any allegiance to the people in the capital. Even though most of us felt we were not the enemy, we realized our continued presence could jeopardize the lives of our friends and hosts. Where would we fit into all of this if a civil war developed? We agreed that we didn't have the skills, the political expertise, or the cultural understanding to answer these questions. But, then, who could have predicted the cataclysm created in the early morning mist?

On Sunday, when I told the students that we might have to abort our study, they were shocked. By

Tuesday, they took it in stride. We discussed alternatives: Should we try to get to Hong Kong by plane or train and wait there to see what would happen? Or should we go directly home? We all agreed that going home was the best solution. With the impetus that comes from making a firm decision, our energy was renewed, even though we knew we'd have to wade through a series of complicated steps before we would be allowed to leave. The program director of the Beijing school was scheduled to return the next morning from an engagement in Europe; it was then that I would tell him we wished to end our program. I knew he would understand.

I spent the rest of the afternoon trying to call home, as I had been doing unsuccessfully since Sunday. The two telephone lines out of the school were perpetually occupied as students hailing from all over the world competed for phones to call relatives, arrange flights, get money, or talk to their embassies.

Eventually, I got through and woke up my husband at four in the morning to tell him that we were secure and planning our exodus. I apologized for interrupting his sleep, explaining that normal daily activity had become so disrupted that I could not call him at a reasonable hour. Dismally, I told him things were not good, but I didn't want to say too much on the phone in case the wires were monitored. Of course I had no way of knowing what he did or didn't know. Even though he said very little, I had the feeling that he knew more than we did and had probably seen a more vivid picture on television than we could imagine. In a hypnotic voice, I said I hoped I would see him again, we still had a long

Beijing: The New Forbidden City

way to go, and the next few days promised to be some of the most difficult for us. When we reached the states, I would call him to arrange the final leg of the trip.

Like fireflies, our brief dance of glory in old Peking was over, our climactic hours of revelry extinguished.

FOREVER YOUNG

Beijing: The New Forbidden City

On our last evening in China, mothers and children strolled within the gates of the compound, stretching their legs and playing with each other. It was one of the first evenings since the massacre that the families living amongst us had ventured outside their homes. The night was serene and reminiscent of happier times.

Restless and needing some air and diversion ourselves, we summoned up enough energy to play with the youngsters. Several of us had packed soap bubbles to give to the children on our trip. Tonight appeared the perfect time to wistfully blow life's breath through fragile soap drawn from fluorescent bottles into laughter at the simplest of things.

Like pied pipers, we soon attracted a bouncing cortege of young children with our tempting trail of fragile spheres. One little boy, about two years old, huffed and puffed so heartily he was never able to form a single bubble. But he remained undaunted, attempt after attempt, as the sticky liquid spilled down his clothes and pooled onto the ground. With a mind of his own, he made his way through the entire jar, resisting our instruction as well as that of his mother. His three-

Forever Young

year-old brother, on the other hand, effortlessly fashioned clouds of the prismatic wonders to our encouraging chorus of "ohs" and "ahs." Another little girl, perhaps about seven, mechanically blew stream after stream of bubbles until she too emptied the whole plastic jar she had claimed as her own.

Once the bottles were drained, we became involved in a lively game of catch with a group of older children. As the play got wilder and wilder, the youngsters squeaked delightfully and the universality of laughter wreathed itself about us, even though we could not communicate with the mothers or children. I kept thinking how difficult it must be for these Chinese parents who nurtured their children, maintaining an atmosphere of peace and regularity, as their hopes and dreams crumbled about them. Would the children ever understand the suffering of their parents? Would they even hear about it? Or would the version of history the party was already rewriting undermine the parents' accounts of the events?

Would these very children strive for the same human rights the "thugs" on the square had espoused, and would they also be crushed because they had been taught that the dreams they had in their hearts were different from those of the "bad" people who had revolted against the common good? Wasn't the culture perpetrating the very friction within itself that it claimed was a result of subversive influences? Would these children be the next generation to fall to the foibles of their leaders?

As the evening peacefully passed, my thoughts turned to my life at home, where I could never feel so fulfilled spending a night simply blowing bubbles. But here, the tension that had built up over the last three days needed to escape. In my enjoyment, I wondered if we had been premature in making our decision to leave. Maybe things were returning to normal? Even if we got stuck here, we'd be able to survive. Somehow the language barrier would be broken down and we'd get to know the people. But then, as a helicopter flew overhead, I realized that the peace, the illusion of normality, and our ability to live within the culture were all as ephemeral as the incandescent bubbles that illuminate a moment only to perish.

FORSAKEN

JUNE 7

Beijing: The New Forbidden City

*A*s Americans, many of us had grown up believing in happy endings. We had come to expect real life to mimic an uncomplicated Steven Spielberg movie, where right inevitably vindicates might. Or maybe it was the mantle of our religious upbringings, which many of us had tossed aside, that made us believe the current impasse was intolerable and would crumble on its own evil foundation. I preferred another explanation: that this tragedy was China's next pivotal axis, and it would prove to be the impetus for its eventual freedom.

At 3:30 A.M., the guns returned, but this time the location and the nature of the gunfire sounded different, almost like some form of retaliation. I did not get up to let anyone know what was going on; they either heard the tanks or they didn't. What could we do anyway? At the end of my emotional rope, drenched in sweat, I froze in my bed. It was too much for me to listen to automatic weapons firing and imagine who was being caught in the cross-fire. Had the "good" soldiers finally arrived to defeat the "bad"? How long would it last? How many nights would Beijing be besieged by its own government? I fretted.

Any reservations I had about leaving China when

Forsaken

we played with the children just a few hours before now vanished. I had to bide time until I could get up and call the embassy at 6:00 A.M. to beg them to come and rescue us as other embassies had done for their citizens. I got up to walk around the room, thinking that if I moved I could infuse my heart's broken spirit with life. Anna, awake in her corner, whispered from her bed that she too could hear the guns and her heart was also racing. Somehow, I felt comforted knowing that another person shared my dismay; it wasn't just my own intrinsic weakness that made me feel so vulnerable.

For the rest of the night, we reviewed our lives like they say one does before death. We spoke to each other about our dreams, our husbands, our disappointments. I told Anna things I had never had the openness to reveal to any other person, including my husband who is my best friend. As an understanding woman and confidant, she became that "safe place" I needed during the long stressful night.

Not even bothering to shower or dress, I shot up at 6:00 A.M. before anyone else had stirred. I stationed myself at the receptionist's booth on our floor and I began calling the American Embassy, repeatedly dialing by hand until the endless ringing on the other end was finally answered and I was connected to the American Citizens' Services. I told them about the gunfire I had heard and asked what had happened during the night. They said there had not been any shooting. I told them again what I had awakened to, but they maintained they were not aware of any turbulence overnight. Maybe they didn't know anything, or perhaps they were trying to keep us from panicking. Apart from our own senses, they were our principle source of information. Were we now going to have to fend for ourselves, since each group seemed to have a different perception of what was going on?

After conferring with the embassy, I went over to the school to meet with the director of the Beijing program who had just returned. Normally restrained and in control, he was furious with what he found upon his return to Beijing. He said no one on his flight of nine passengers landing in Beijing had heard anything about what was really going on in China. He said if he had known, he would not have returned to his country. I couldn't believe his words. This Chinese acquaintance was the epitome of responsibility, nationalist pride, and love of family. His declaration that he would not have returned to his position, homeland, or loved ones if he had been aware of what had occurred on the morning of June 4 indicated to me that China's domestic conflict was far from over.

Even though I had gone over to school to tell him we wanted to be freed from our contract, I politely asked his advice about what to do. "Yes, yes, go, go. Nothing but trouble is here. There will be food and fuel shortages soon. You will not be allowed back in the hospitals. You cannot trust talking to anyone. Your lives could be in danger. Yes, it is time to go, as soon as possible," he divulged, looking as though his florid face would explode.

With my task accomplished, I went back to the dorm to assemble the group and tell them what had happened the night before and what I had accomplished so far that morning. I needed them all to help with the arrangements to go home. I called the American Embassy again to relay our plans, since they wanted to keep track of U.S. citizens in China. I disclosed that our strategy was to get to the airport and wait until we could get a flight. We realized we might have to fly stand-by or even wait for days, but our impression was that the airport was safe. It seemed to make sense to go to the airport instead of hiding in the abandoned dorm; after all, it would put us one step closer to home.

The embassy told me I was crazy and that the best thing we could do was to stay put. We were safe, weren't we? They refused to come get us at our residence but said they would pick us up if we got to Beijing University or Kentucky Fried Chicken, and from there they would take us to the Jianguo Hotel. Flabbergasted, I told them it was common knowledge that those were three of the most dangerous locations in the city. Didn't they realize that just the night before students had been slaughtered at Beijing University? We could not consciously enter dangerous territory. Recognizing my resolve, they finally recommended that we immediately make airline reservations. They also contended we would never get out of the airport without repurchasing new tickets, precious pieces of paper promising freedom.

Unlike American airports, where you can purchase tickets or ask for information, there are no comparable services at the Beijing airport. So we started calling every airline that flew into Beijing to see if we could purchase new tickets. Monopolizing the two phones for hours, we called each airline over and over again, trying to catch a free interval between the incessant busy signals. If looks could kill, I would have been dead many times over from the fiendish stares of other people waiting to use the phones. But I had been cooperative and patient long enough. We were leaving that day, with or without anybody's help.

With Robert and Lynsay acting as relays between the two phone locations, Dairne and I were able to coordinate our reservations. She got through first and booked enough tickets to get us out of the city with United Airlines on a flight to Tokyo. I called the American Embassy back to let them know that we would be able to leave, and asked if they could give us a ride to the Tower Building close to the Jianguo Hotel to pick up the tickets. Again, after I described where we were living, they quite flatly said they couldn't help us. With all respect and appreciation of their difficult task, I again begged them to come and get us. The woman with whom I was speaking finally acknowledged in a frigid voice, "Your group is too small to come and get. You are in a dangerous sector of the city. Our advice is that either you stay put or get out as best you can. There are eight thousand Americans in China and you are only eight of them. You're on our own. Good luck."

As a "spoiled" American, I could not fathom her position. Too small to come and get? Was even one American too small a number to be rescued? Such was my belief in the preeminence of the individual. Incredulously, I repeated her words to Dairne, as I scribbled the quote down on paper as if to convince myself that this was really happening. We had been forsaken.

FELLOWSHIP

Beijing: The New Forbidden City

*U*nder such far-fetched circumstances, our responses became frenetic. Dairne began calling other embassies, beseeching them to help us in our desperation. She called the Swiss, German, French and even Soviet agencies to no avail; their lines were also hopelessly busy. I ran over to the school to tell the administration that our government said they could not assist us and we needed their help now. While everyone's' fuses became progressively shorter, they said they could do nothing for us and insisted we call the American Embassy back and <u>make</u> them responsible for our safe return.

As I dejectedly retraced my path back to the dorm, the Brazilian envoy pulled up to evacuate one girl from their country studying at the institute. Surprising them with my fluent Portuguese, I entreated them to take the six of us to the airport. Even though their mini-van was empty, they claimed they could not help us, adding that they they were also seeking help from the American Embassy to evacuate Brazilian citizens from China. This confirmed our fears that we had been abandoned.

Back in the dorm, we decided someone had to go out on the streets to pick up the tickets. The rest of us

Fellowship

would pack everything and continue trying to arrange transportation to the airport. Lynsay and Anna, anxious to help and restless from confinement, volunteered to take their bikes out on the streets and ride to the center of town to arrange our passage home. Hastily, we gathered in my room, collecting all the dollars we could to buy new tickets, and doling out last-minute instructions on cautious behavior. Within minutes, the duo departed with our Chinese guide who insisted on accompanying them. We were all glad there had been no problem in obtaining volunteers, for the rest of us had no desire to leave the premises, especially unprotected on bikes.

Dairne continued to dial the list of embassies located in Beijing while the rest of us, working in pairs, scurried through the dorm packing the belongings of Anna, Lynsay, Stan, and Gigi, in anticipation of our imminent departure. Unhesitatingly, I ripped the journal notes from my travel diary and pinned the pages inside the hems of my skirts and dresses buried deep within my bag, along with my *Victor* button.

During the bustle of departing, we heard from the American Embassy. Perhaps as a condolence, the spokesperson suggested she might be able to get us a bus to go to the airport if I was willing to drive. I told her, if worse came to worse, we might have to accept her offer, but for now, it would not be prudent for me to transport my classmates through the unknown, rabble-ridden, tank-lined, closed off streets of Beijing. I politely declined her offer.

Everything happened so fast during that hectic

afternoon. Suddenly, a messenger bolted up the stairs to our third floor wing and told us that a bus would be in the courtyard within a few minutes to take us to the Holiday Inn on the outskirts of town for the night. This was our only chance to leave. We automatically formed a human chain down the two flights of stairs, and hoisted our heavy luggage onto the growling bus. The Chinese attendants on the second floor, who always checked our keys, huddled about the receptionist's desk with obvious excitement over our exodus. They could see our conflicting emotions as we grappled not only with our fears, but also with our attachment to their country, a place we were heartbroken to leave.

Our last bags were stowed on the van along with those of several other friends who had booked rooms at the Holiday Inn. They generously invited us to share their reserved quarters with them. Dairne offered to stay behind in the deserted dorm to await the return of Anna and Lynsay, so they would know where we had gone. Breathlessly, we parted. Our group was progressively becoming fragmented. Would we all rendezvous later that day? Would the same group that had excitedly journeyed together to this mysterious land be allowed to depart together?

Surprisingly, all of the significant personages on staff with our program gathered outside our private quarters to wish us well on the rest of the venture we would have to make without them. Tears welled up in their eyes as they bittersweetly bade us goodbye. They almost seemed embarrassed that we, their guests, were no longer welcome in their homeland. Endeavoring to express our gratitude for their aid and our continuing feelings of kinship for them, I chirped hopefully, "*Mingnian*, next year," with tears rolling down my pale cheeks. "*Mingnian*," they breathed, whispering the words like a fervent prayer, bowing, then proudly raising their shining eyes to meet mine.

Someday, perhaps "next year," some of us would return to show our abiding love for the Chinese people and the best their culture had to offer. Temporarily, we must leave this beloved country. An inevitable revolution was bound to explode when the people would no longer accept the oppression mandated by a small group of leaders.

There had never been any doubt in my mind that the very event that signified the temporary denial of democracy in China, that had taken away the lives of their children, would also mark the demise of the regime and christen those martyrs forever young in the flames of freedom.

We pulled out of the secure gates of the compound, leaving our fleet of gaily-graced bikes behind us. Thrusting a handful of keys into the pocket of our bus driver, I told him (aided by one of the students from England who was of Chinese descent) to sell the bikes or use them for the movement. He kept promising that he would sell them and send us the money, but I shook my head. We were leaving them behind. Our precious used bikes were never ours to start and, now, China was reclaiming them with a bloody hand.

Burying myself in the back of the bus, I put my head down in my arms and sighed out my grief. Our normally buoyant group was silent as the vehicle conducted us through detoured streets conspicuously devoid of normal commerce, bicycles, and people, littered with strips of rubber, twisted steel, and abandoned vehicles.

It was the first time we had seen the streets since the massacre. Hunched down in my seat, I kept my eyes directed straight ahead, not daring to appear curious, but I stretched my peripheral vision as far as it would take me. Soldiers stood along the tree-lined boulevards, clutching rifles in their arms as they talked to small groups of citizens in the shade. The bus driver told us they were the "good" soldiers, come to keep peace in the city constrained by martial law and curfew, metal and megalomania, death and desperation. Beijing never looked so barren.

*FOXHOLE
IN
FANTASY LAND*

Beijing: The New Forbidden City

The familiar green and white emblem of the hotel set back off the airport road peaked out from lush country foliage. We had arrived unscathed to the comfort of a welcome institution, the Lido Holiday Inn. As our anxious bus driver pulled up alongside the entrance, we hurriedly began throwing baggage off the panting vehicle. With the newly imposed curfew, we knew our nervous friend needed to leave as soon as possible.

Pools of tears sprang from his eyes while his down-turned mouth expressed his sorrow when we said good-bye to this courageous friend who had risked his life volunteering to take us to a safe abode. Thrusting one thousand yuan (about $250.00) into his hands, I said, "This is for the students." His only protest was to hang his head, a symbol of the severity of the circumstances, for normally the Chinese would vociferously refuse even the simplest gesture of generosity. "*Mingnian*, next year," I swallowed. It was easier, more hopeful than saying goodbye, as his drooping look of finality singed my soul.

We managed to transport our cumbersome luggage into the luxurious lobby of the Holiday Inn. Once within the heavy glass doors of our new fortress, I breathed a sigh of relief: We were safe. As if in a trance, I stood tending the bags mounted in a trolley cart while Martha and Gilbert checked us into the hotel.

The Holiday Inn was always a must on any trip to Beijing. The previous year it had served as a refuge on more than one occasion when the surrealism of China became too much for us. Every other weekend, we surpassed even our normal American insouciance venting pent-up energy dancing at Glorianna's nightclub. To the rhythm of the top forties, we would challenge each other with our gyrations, demonstratively swaying alongside staid, wealthy Overseas Chinese who seemed oddly out of place in the upbeat disco. It certainly never occurred to me then that this festive Holiday Inn would have to serve as a stepping stone to freedom on the night before our evacuation from the country.

Although things were essentially as I remembered them, with the imposing chandelier flickering in a lobby flanked by tropical fronds, the overall effect was disorienting. Somehow, our arrival at a hotel reveling in its own internal life of music, marble, and brass, was overwhelming in contrast to all that we had just been through. What we had accepted last year as normal American comfort was now a never-never land of fairytale fantasy. Just as in the last few days the unreal had become real, now the real seemed surreal.

Stoically, I stood by the luggage cart, disheveled, depressed and disorganized, feeling like I had been beamed up to Disneyland from another reality in the blink of an eye. Beneath one roof were all the accoutrements of American culture — a pizza parlor, bowling alley, swimming pool, coffee shop, bars, three restaurants, beauty parlor, gift stores, and a disco — diversion in every direction, services any American would automatically expect in a reputable hotel. But we had just passed through rabble-ridden streets lined with soldiers and tanks, barren avenues devoid of bicycle traffic where potential death seemed to lurk at every corner. Clinking glasses of fine liquors and the liberating disco rhythms may have muffled the moans of injustice smothering in the city, but my being was still vibrating from the transition. Which apparition was real? How could such simultaneous, contiguous realities exist? Would anyone who hadn't seen what we had only glimpsed ever understand our reality, much less that of the condemned citizens?

Checking in took a long time because the lobby was overflowing with a variety of international tourists who created a teeming Tower of Babel. Finally we secured keys and were escorted to our $120.00-a-night accommodations. After we had divided the luggage between the two rooms the eight of us would share, one for the men and one for the women, I instinctively gravitated to the television set, lusting for the electronic window to the world that might enlighten us.

The replay of the heart-stopping scene when a lone Chinese citizen challenged the column of tanks appeared like a mirage. Hand to heart, I could not believe the specter staged in front of my eyes, the forces of good and evil aligned face to face. I had no idea what would occur. But when I witnessed his bravery, and that of the friends who rescued him, I was again convinced that someday, as a result of courageous stances like this in the face of a bloodbath, liberty would blossom in China once again. Good would prevail.

Anna was still with Lynsay purchasing our passes to freedom. Dairne, I imagined, was pacing the prison-like dorm, an animal waiting to be sprung free. Stan and Gigi were still at the hospital. Although it was the middle of June, I was freezing cold. I turned off the air conditioner and drew myself a hot bath to warm up.

In my overwrought emotional state, even the bathroom overwhelmed me. Stark black and white tiles seemed to grin tauntingly, along with shimmering chrome and porcelain appointments, towels as soft and white as clouds, and gleaming crystal-clear water glasses. Its opulence was unfamiliar and out of proportion to the world we had inhabited for thirteen short days. Was no comfort to be found here as well?

While I waited for my bath to fill, I gobbled up a bag of peanuts and poured myself a soft drink from the little refrigerator in our bedroom. Taking the soda into the bathroom, I sank into the warmth of the tub, hoping that the soothing hot liquid would purge my mind. Like water desiring to return to its source, my hollow tears noiselessly blended with the bath water. Even though I closed my eyes, I could not stop seeing the tragic streets.

I emerged from the tub still exhausted and disappointingly unfortified to begin the telethon of phone calls that awaited me. Worried about the others, I realized that the seductive semblance of serenity the hotel room comforts might have provided was still elusive. First, I called the embassy to let them know that most of us had managed to get to the hotel but the rest of our friends still needed a ride. I also called the school to let them know we had been safely transported to the hotel.

Soon, Dairne frantically burst into the room, accompanied by our head translator. She hurriedly told us that Anna and Lynsay had somehow become separated from our translator when the three of them went to purchase the airline tickets. Now the two others were alone in the city and no one knew their whereabouts. We also learned that our bus driver, who had been on his way home after dropping us off at the hotel, made Dairne leave the dorm when he found out the others had been lost. Violating curfew and courageously undertaking another forbidden journey in our behalf, he insisted upon returning her to the fold.

Our concern for Anna and Lynsay, who were somewhere out on the streets, mounted until we were quite anxious. Suddenly Lynsay called. After he and Anna had secured the tickets, he explained, they went to the American Embassy close to the Tower Building, hoping that a personal visit would be more effective in inducing embassy personnel to pick us up at the dorm. But the American Embassy claimed that, even though they had enough buses, all of their Chinese drivers had quit. In the interim, they deposited Lynsay and Anna at the Jianguo Hotel close to the embassy along the dangerous Jianguomennei intersection.

We were happy to know where they were, but we wanted them to reunite with us. One last time, our stalwart bus driver agreed to pick up another contingent of our group. By early evening, Lynsay and Anna returned and we were all together again, except for Stan and Gigi who were still at the hospital. We were almost ready to leave.

My friends said a final tearful goodbye to our translator/host who had become our friend. Accompanying him outside of the room, I thanked him for his invaluable aid, pressing a string of seeds and turquoise into the handshake he extended. "These are called ghost beads," I chanted. "The Indians used them for protection from evil spirits. Let them protect you from any evil you may be forced to endure," I explained, as I turned over the protective beads I had purchased for our safety before leaving the states. "Yes, thank you," he said. Stuffing them into his pockets, he turned his head back and forth in the hotel hall, checking to see if anyone had seen him covertly conspiring with an American.

I knew he took no stock in what I had said. Previously, when we had discussions on religion, God, good and evil, I was amazed at his frankly logical conclusion that there could be no God. The party, he had been taught, would bring heaven to earth. Yet they had lied throughout his whole life. How could he believe in the promises of an unseen god when the ever visible party bent their social platitudes in favor of every personal opportunity?

Calling the American Embassy again, we entreated them to pick up our last two friends at the hospital. We repeated what the doctors had told us: Gigi could travel if it was absolutely necessary even though she was still very weak and required more blood. The embassy maintained that they could not go into the district where Stan and Gigi had been since Monday morning because it was much too perilous with active fighting still going on.

Finally, we convinced them we meant business: We were going tomorrow as a group, with or without their help. After much protest, an embassy official agreed to pick up Stan and his wife the next morning and bring them to the airport to join us. Although we weren't happy with the arrangement, we realized we didn't have too many options, so we contacted Stan and told him the plans and that we would see him and Gigi the next day.

After a scanty, expensive meal in the hotel's Chinese dining room, we retired to our quarters. Shortly thereafter, as we were sorting our bags and getting settled for the night, Stan appeared at the door. Following our phone conversation, the "never tired" Stan had decided he was not going to put his life or Gigi's into anyone else's hands. After what seemed an interminable rigmarole, he had paid the hospital bill and carried his fragile wife in his arms to a taxi stand, where for one hundred yuan, a resourceful driver's services were obtained.

Things were coming together. Three more legs of the journey remained - the night, the expedition to the airport, and the final departure.

Two-to-a-bed, we prepared to rest, but I already knew I wouldn't be able to sleep. Right before turning off the lights, we decided to watch the news one more time. After the sequences on China, the coverage turned to world news. We were surprised to hear that the Ayatollah Khomeini had died, and we watched in silence as hysterical mourners encroached upon his grey, shrouded body like a swarm of ants. But then, when his corpse unexpectedly tumbled off his bier with his subjects throwing themselves upon him in despair, we collectively laughed for the first time in days. The incongruity of the lamentation coupled with the falling body catalyzed our repressed tensions. Death was not so final and ugly after all. What mattered was who we had been and what we had left behind.

FRENZY

JUNE 8

Beijing: The New Forbidden City

The night was as long as an Antarctic day. Restlessly biding time in the stifling room, we tried to sleep. Throughout the endless night, I could hear the drone of tanks stealthily crawling into the city via the airport road, hidden under the blanket of darkness. Would we be barricaded from leaving? Would we make it to the airport? Would we survive the night?

As my heart did acrobatics, I tried to reconcile myself to the possibility that we could be killed. When Anna and I had discussed the possibility of death a few mornings before, our conversation had quelled our fears. But now, I lie grappling with the possibility alone. The truth was, I didn't want to die. Although my body felt spent at this moment, I saw myself as young and vital. I had things to do, my life's work, my mission. What would be the purpose of dying? Could the murder of Americans in China alter the totalitarian regime? Could our deaths bring life to that country? Would we be casualties of being in the wrong place at the wrong time?

My greatest sadness was that my parents would grieve and think I had been a victim. I wanted them to know that if I was harmed, it really was alright. My life had been rich, full of love, affection, achievement, purpose, and potential. The life they gave me, that made me who I was, had been possible because of the freedom governing my homeland and the way they had allowed me to grow and discover myself within that freedom. Giving up my life would attest to the value of everything they had taught me. If I could help this country that I loved, and further the cause of freedom that was my birthright, it would be alright. I just wanted to go to my death without fear.

As I wrestled with my mortality, sweat percolated through my pores, stealing my strength. When would morning come? At 5:00 A.M., the alarm riveted my worn-out form. My roommates and I dressed and packed mechanically, each absorbed in our own thoughts. Was I the only one who was afraid? I needed to ground myself, yet, not wanting to upset the others, I refrained from asking anyone how they felt. Finally packed, I only needed my lipstick. I knew I had carefully placed it in one of the pouches of my backpack, but it eluded me this morning. Repeatedly, I packed and unpacked my bag looking for it, feeling I needed my lipstick to get us out of the country.

I began thinking about how, before I left on my trip, a friend of mine who entertained me one evening after a meeting, had revealed a hidden talent of his by offering to do a numerological reading. I listened skeptically as he prophesied that my path was to pursue knowledge at any expense. He likened me to a warrior, attired in stunning silk, who would lead people into battle. And they would follow me anywhere, such was my conviction, even if I was wrong. Clarity, he declared, would come from having intent. When I lacked intent, however, an amethyst stone could aid me. He claimed that my personal power was derived from how I was perceived and, therefore, I should never go out of the house unless I looked my best, no matter what that meant.

Flattered by the image but skeptical of its substance, I filed his revelation away. However, when I was packing for China, I did put an amethyst crystal in my jeans pocket, and from my collection of earrings, selected some amethyst crystals to dangle close to my brain. Thinking of his words this morning in connection with our own battle, I felt I must wear my lipstick, the insignia of my personal power. Frantically, I searched for the tube of pigment, but it was futile. Maybe it was time for me to get rid of this cultural crutch and learn to rely on what was inside instead of pretense. Abandoning the quest, I resolved that our fate would not be jeopardized because I couldn't find my lipstick.

Convening in the lobby at 6:00 A.M., we checked out of the hotel and then gathered for some breakfast before grabbing the shuttle to the airport. A typical American buffet was being served —pancakes, sausage, muffins, bacon, and eggs. How could anyone eat? I felt sullen, scared, and subdued. Although the food repulsed me, I forced myself to nibble on a slice of rye toast and swallow a cup of tea. Everyone was eating like it was just another meal. Finally, I blurted out, "Isn't anyone else afraid?" "Yes," several chimed in, "but what can we do about it?" We all had to go through the motions that would get us out of the country. This could be our last meal for awhile. Who knew what we would encounter when we reached the airport?

One last time before leaving, some of the women went to the Ladies' room. A little old woman was wiping sparkling marble counters and straightening dainty hand towels. It was customary in the fancy hotels to give the bathroom attendant a small tip for keeping the restroom fresh and pleasant. As we left several of my friends each pressed a fifty yuan bill into her grateful hands (about $12.00). With a quivering smile, she raised her tear-filled eyes in gratitude.

So many tourists were leaving that morning that the hotel had to provide two large touring buses to transport everyone to the airport. Stan opted to hire a taxi for him and Gigi so she would not be crushed by the ardent crowd. The rest of us were divided between the two buses.

Uneventfully, the coach flashed down the airport road, as fog condensing above the rich farmland meandered through the quiet countryside. No signs of tanks or troops were visible. The governmental fangs must be securely clenched on the heart of the dragon, I thought.

Standing with Lynsay on the crowded bus, I had to concentrate to keep myself from fainting as we headed toward our destination. Surprisingly, the airport was virtually empty when we arrived. The throngs we had expected to encounter there had apparently been rescued. We were relieved. After passing through customs fairly quickly, we tried to decide where to get in line with all of our luggage. Because it was so early, our flight had not yet been posted. For the time being, we collapsed on our load, already tired from the activities of the morning, not to mention a night of sleeplessness. Steadily, the airport began to swell with people eager to leave. Gigi, weak from her own personal ordeal, was surrounded by crowds who were not always considerate of her frail, withered body.

As airport personnel began to arrive, signs were posted heralding the lines for flights to Hong Kong, San Francisco, Tokyo, and New York. Organization became almost impossible as the growing crowd clamored towards the counters with handfuls of money, passports, and tickets waving in the air. Oriental men dressed in business suits, shouting and pushing uncontrollably, climbed on top of each others' backs and then up onto the counter, only to meet the restraining arms of the ticket counter personnel. We could hardly believe our eyes. Although we had all experienced chaotic scenes before, we had never witnessed such mayhem as this.

Our goal was to leave that day. We did not have the stamina to persist beyond a few hours, although we fully expected to watch several flights leave without us, or to be claimed one-by-one going stand-by. Everyone's energy was needed to coordinate the difficult task of getting us out of the airport, so we divided our resources. I appointed Anna to stand in the queue for China Airline (CAAC) in the hope that they would accept our original tickets, booked with them for the end of June in exchange for a flight that day. Stan joined her since we had not secured alternate tickets for him and Gigi, not knowing whether they would be able to leave with us or not. I stood in the stand-by line for the United Airlines Tokyo

Frenzy

flight for which Anna and Lynsay had bought tickets the day before. Robert ran to get me a Coke and some chocolate to keep me from fainting in the hot, converging line of evacuees. Lynsay communicated between all the parties, updating us on each others' progress.

We really didn't want to go to Tokyo because when we arrived there we would have to find a flight to San Francisco and the whole ordeal would be prolonged. Back at the dorm, we had heard that CAAC would not honor our tickets. I found that hard to believe, but while we were at the airport, we ran into some friends of ours from Santa Fe on another study tour who confirmed that they had spent the night at the airport and had to repurchase tickets because CAAC would not accept their pre-purchased tickets.

While waiting in the United Airlines line, Americans began sharing stories with each other. We spoke with several young exchange students studying at Beijing University who told us they had watched their Chinese classmates slain before their very eyes. They too had been shot at as they hid behind bushes on campus. Some planned to go to Hong Kong for several weeks and lie low, waiting for a safe time to return to Beijing. Others declared they would never feel safe coming back.

Our names were still quite a way down on the stand-by list, about fifty more names were ahead of us, but since we had arrived at the airport early, I was hoping we would secure a flight by mid-afternoon. Suddenly Dairne came running to rescue Lynsay, Robert, and I. "You're going," she yelled. "Anna got through and has seats on CAAC! The plane is waiting for you now." Her words didn't sink in. Stalwartly, I remained at the front of the line where I was persistently making my way. "Come on, come on, you're going to San Francisco now," she repeated triumphantly. "You're going home."

FAREWELL TO A FIELD OF DREAMS

Beijing: The New Forbidden City

After scurrying through customs, everyone but Dairne dashed onto the plane. It was her decision to go to Tokyo and from there travel to other places in the Orient, but we still felt guilty leaving her behind. In roughly three short hours, we had secured our evacuation from the country, fleeing like Bedouins from a sudden storm. Even the previous year, under normal conditions, we had been detained in the airport for eleven hours while a broken engine was being repaired.

We collapsed in the last few seats on the plane that had not been reserved to pick up passengers in Shanghai. The routinism of everything on the plane was disconcerting, but it was also preparing us for what was to come upon our return to the United States. As I retreated into my own emotional thoughts, tears saturated my eyes, half out of gratitude that the group was safe, half out of sorrow for the circumstances dictating our departure. Sitting alone by the window, I gazed out onto the concrete bastion of the airport where it appeared to be just another normal day.

As the plane prepared to depart, I bid my private adieu to China. Would I ever have the chance to return? Would groups like ours ever have the opportunity to

Farewell to a Field of Dreams

study here again? Here we were, being comfortably catered to inside a metal bird, as dentist music mixed with the aroma of airline coffee drifted down the aisles. We were being rescued from the post-crackdown clean-up that was bound to follow the massacre. It seemed unfair that money and national background afforded us the privilege to exit.

Across the aisle from me, a young Chinese man dressed in a poorly-made business suit looked as heartbroken as I felt. After exchanging sympathetic glances, we began to talk. He told me he had gone down to the American Embassy to try to get visas for three friends but was only granted one. He thought the process was unfair and arbitrary and I wondered what forces had ordained that the favored dark man, sitting with apprehension by his side, should be the one saved.

The jet oriented itself to the east, taking off into the infinite grey emptiness that awaited us. Conflicting feelings flooded me as the gauzy mist extended its gentle fingers as if in one last lingering embrace. Then, kindly, the mist parted to provide a final look at the People's Republic.

Luscious fields of green foliage rolled in every direction, and I could see small huts, wooden carts, and brown bodies. The tanks and wreckage were hidden from my view. Instead, I saw ample crops maturing in the summer sun coming to fruition under the beneficent hand of nature. Their tenants, minding the bounty, seemed to live within its shadows amidst a field of dreams. Then like Jonah in the belly of the whale, we were swallowed by the sky.

195

FLYING TIGERS

Beijing: The New Forbidden City

Sitting on the plane, I thought back over the previous year's journey when members of our group had chosen to depart on different days. I recalled how later, when we all got together again in the states, a friend had entertained us with the story of his departure from China. Just before take-off, he relayed, the flight attendant in charge announced that the first fifteen rows of passengers needed to go to the back of the plane in order for the aircraft to lift off. Apparently, the plane was too heavy up front, so everyone sauntered warily to the rear of the plane where they stood as its wheels lifted from the earth. Recalling his humorous tale, I found it almost as unbelievable as our tragic fate.

Leaning back in the seat I would occupy for the next thirteen hours, my only respite was to close my eyes. I was awakened from my reverie an hour later when we touched down in ever-grey Shanghai to pick up more passengers and have our visas checked.

While Martha and I got a soft drink in the cocktail lounge, Lynsay and Anna scouted the shopping counters one last time. Coming upon the Christian Dior lipstick display with its inviting shades of burnished roses and tropical sunsets, they considered buying one for me.

Independently, I had considered doing the same thing, but heroically decided not to since the worst was over and I had survived without my crutch. Like a nomad crossing the Nile, I had only needed what was necessary.

When we got back on the plane, I recalled how, on my last trip, the airliner had been secretly invaded by a multitude of mosquitoes after we had checked out of the country. The smell of our sweet flesh and the hot, heavy air must have lured the marauders. In a frenzy, passengers began spraying cans of insect repellant in the closed cabin, and I vividly remembered choking on the noxious fumes. All night long, the mosquitos hummed over bare legs and necks, ears and feet, attacking at every opportunity. The sound of newspapers slapping in the darkened hatch spliced the night. When the morning sun peeked into the plane, it revealed a trail of blood and transparent wings spattered all over the white wall of the cabin.

Another midnight murder, I reflected. No mosquitoes awaited us when we re-boarded the jet this time, perhaps because it was still daytime, but I couldn't help but revisit last year's bloody invasion in my weary mind.

I dozed off between the repeated service of food and drinks. My spirit was tired and I did not want to talk. When Working Girl and Cocoon II, the two movies we had seen just two weeks before on our trip over to China, appeared on the screen again, I watched them through half-open, tiger-like eyes, ferociously clinging to their visions of hope.

FUTURE

JUNE 8

Beijing: The New Forbidden City

*E*xhausted and disoriented, we touched down at the San Francisco airport to greet a clapping and cheering crowd. But my heart was still heavy, my mind in China. Numbly, we passed through customs into a barrage of photographers' flashes and reporters' microphones thrust into our faces. The press was anxious to hear our first-hand account of our escape from Beijing. Their queries, however, were centered upon the role of the American Embassy, of which they already seemed informed, and not on personal experiences in the besieged capital. While we were happy to be cooperative, we were also anxious to get on with the last part of our journey. Heading home, we looked forward to soon being able to settle into some semblance of normalcy.

After the reporters became satiated with my version of the story, I started to make my cumbersome way, luggage in tow, to the appropriate ticket counter where I hoped to secure the next connecting flight home. As I disengaged myself from their electrical lair, my peripheral vision took in two tall, overweight Chinese men with taunting smiles on their dark faces. A momentary thought crossed my mind: How ironic it would be if I had survived all of the turmoil in Beijing only to find danger at this final juncture of the trip. Casting my eyes downward and picking up my pace, I uneasily headed for the escalator. I sighed in relief only after I was sure I had cleared their purview. Suddenly, a hand gripped my shoulder. For the first time in the four nights since I first heard the bullets felling the Chinese children, I released my pent up feelings and screamed. Terrified, I turned to find that the hand belonged to the Chinese man with whom I had silently cried as we took off from Beijing. Tears filled his eyes and an eager smile crossed his tragic face as he implored, with uncharacteristic Chinese emotion, "Did you tell your story?" Relieved that it was him, and finally becoming aware that I was in America, I breathed freely and replied, "Yes, I told my story."

*FINALE
AFTER THE
FALL FROM HEAVEN*

Beijing: The New Forbidden City

*T*he night was as dark as a Russian's glance, the stars his glinting eyes. The crisp clean air, devoid of citrine clouds of smoke, rushed into my lungs. Ah... freedom's fragrance! As we drove up from a small valley that had temporarily obscured the view of Santa Fe, an American flag preened in the moonlight, reveling in its own nakedness, stark and surreal against the mountain-defined sky. The flag's cluster of stars, gleaming from its eye of blue, met my gaze, and brilliant red stripes, like friendly lips, smiled in welcome. The colors of life, the colors of freedom seemed to envelop me. I truly felt there was no place like home.

The morning after my first night of solid sleep, a peaceful rest no longer laced with sirens or bullets, I was greeted by stacks of phone messages, newspapers, and magazines. Where to begin?

In one pile, I found a letter from my sister telling me how she had tried to explain to her children what was going on in China after they saw some news bulletins on TV. The eldest, Anthony, a precocious boy of six, had seen a label on some clothing that said "Made in China." He wanted to know: "How do they have time to make things in China when they're having a war?"

Finale - After The Fall From Heaven

While I can't claim the same naive inquisitiveness as Anthony, I still wonder nine months later, as I finish this book, how many personal sparks of human consciousness were needed to spark a greater light of freedom in China. When will the Middle Kingdom find the middle road between Mao and modernization, Deng and his dual messages of socialism and the back door? When will *fengshui*, "the proper relationship between things," be reestablished in a country that gave birth to this philosophical heritage?

Several weeks later, I found myself still disturbed by my thirteen days in Beijing. My spirit was crushed; I felt like a caged bird that couldn't find fulfillment in familiar surroundings. Then, one morning, as I gazed out of our living room window at a palette of flowers that my husband had planted while I was away, now embraced in diamond-faceted sunshine, a hummingbird, rare to the Santa Fe terrain, appeared before my eyes. Filled with wonder over its magnificence, I stood transfixed. The tiny bird paused just long enough over a sweet cluster of flowers as if to say everything would be alright. Life was good, beautiful, magical, and mysterious. My fluttering visitor seemed to be affirming that someday China would recover from its fall from heaven and the Chinese people would know peaceful freedom once again. In that moment, the hole I had fallen into in my heart filled with hope and serenity and I felt mended. Life's spirit returned and my view of the world was restored.

THE END

FOOTNOTES

Beijing: The New Forbidden City

It has been several moons since "mingnian." I am still obsessed with China, and feeling broken because we have decided not to return there until some reconciliation can be made with the government. I continue to saturate my consciousness with the contradictions that are China, voraciously reading, studying, writing, and sermonizing, as I struggle to gain a perspective on the significance of the Tiananmen Massacre. Cautioning myself not to be reactionary or romantic, I am carefully considering the political implications of resuming relationships with that recalcitrant country.

As a sociologist, I have tried to justify a return visit, reasoning that a resumption of relationships would confirm my belief that social change occurs from the grass-roots up. As a person, I feel that the horror of June 4 was as unholy as the Nazi holocaust that continues to scar personal, social, national, and human history. Periodically, immersing myself in a novel about Chinese life, I get caught up in images of mountains, the Forbidden City, or street life, and I remember the peace of the Llama Temple and the golden Buddha of the Future, the frivolity of the Lantern Festival, and the toothless smiles of the people. Then I am almost seduced into ignoring the political standstill in favor of my personal needs.

With the economic resources of China virtually untapped, it is easy to see why multinational moguls, as lured by the riches of that nation as Marco Polo, ignore what abhorred the world just one year ago. I am sure that the bottom line behind the smiles and handshakes we see extended on the evening news is greed. It's easy to avert one's eyes from uncomfortable facts when dollar signs, as numerous as the bowls of rice consumed daily by over a billion people, proliferate.

Being an optimist with an unflagging belief in the essential goodness of man, I was brought up to believe that the world would never forget the atrocities of World War II. From The Diary of Anne Frank to War and Remembrances, I cannot fathom that our social conscience will ever permit us to forget the slaughter, round-up, and persecution of innocent people.

My cultural naivete was so great that, when we saw the news for the first time on television at the Holiday Inn, my immediate reaction was that President Bush, with his love of China and political acumen in that area, would somehow find a way to make peace with the perpetrators and bring about a reconciliation between the two countries. But one year later, as Eastern countries unexpectedly fall like dominoes in the direction of democracy, our amends with China have not been made.

Some businesses are sneaking back into China today. International relations go on in secret over polite toasts. But the thumbs of hard-liners Li Peng and dying Deng Xiaoping continue to obstruct the pulse of everyday life.

Beijing: The New Forbidden City

I entreat the governments of the world to rise above their own political and economic agendas, their own pieces of the pie, to see the bigger picture of the stifled human spirit that stands at the gate of heavenly peace.

**New Books By The Author
To Be Released In 1991:**

HOLDING THE TIGER'S TAIL
and
THE MAGIC HAND RETURNS SPRING